TIPPING

for

SUCCESS!

TIPPING

for

SUCCESS!

*Secrets for How to Get In
and Get Great Service*

MARK L. BRENNER

Brenmark House
13333 Ventura Boulevard
Sherman Oaks, California 91423
Tel: 818-986-2500 Fax: 818-986-3636
Web: www.brenmarkhouse.com

Cover and Interior Design:
Peri Poloni, Knockout Design <www.knockoutbooks.com>

Gail Kearns, Editor

ISBN No. 0-9708766-3-7
Library of Congress Preassigned Catalog No. 00-193537

The New Yorker Collection cartoons with permission by
The Cartoon Bank, a division of *The New Yorker* Magazine.

Hotel front desk with permission by Luxe Hotel Rodeo Drive,
Beverly Hills, California

Printed in the United States.

10 9 8 7 6 5 4 3 2 1

Dedicated to my grandfather

who unwittingly taught me the

gentle *art* of tipping.

TABLE OF CONTENTS

ACKNOWLEDGMENTS

A special thanks to the hundreds of professional service providers who have contributed to my research for this book. I also would like to give special mention to those whom I've had the pleasure to get to know, as well as the pleasure of receiving your great hospitality, thanks so much. Finally, to the remaining millions of professionals who truly value the customer and who pride themselves on making the customer's experience a satisfying one. I salute all of you and remain grateful.

About the Author

It's no coincidence my three professional pursuits—the study of human behavior, business enterprise, and sleight of hand magic—have unexpectedly played a unique role in writing this book. I began my career more than 20 years ago as a behaviorist and family therapist. Those experiences led me to new insights regarding patterns of human behavior based on the social influence process.

During that time, I also became keenly interested in the secret and elusive world of close-up magic—both as a performer and observer of how people react to the art of presentation and the science of illusion. I began to perform professionally and appear at the famous Magic Castle in Hollywood. Magic had become a great reminder in the power of believing in oneself. A magician, like an entrepreneur, cannot make his audience believe anything unless he believes in it himself. Like tipping, magic requires an honest confidence. That is, the art of presenting an idea or yourself in a formidable way. My own personal measure as a performer was put to the test one evening when I learned the great Marlon Brando was in the audience, and I might add, in the front row. Unless I had full confidence in my skills and the belief in my performance, the audience would never suspend their own powers of logic. I must have done well. Weeks later I received a personal call from Mr. Brando, inviting me to perform at a private affair he was hosting.

Over these past 25 years, I've written many books, and have founded numerous innovative companies bringing to the marketplace leading edge products ranging from consumer electronics to Internet information services. As I look back, it becomes quite clear that my entrepreneurial ventures were largely influenced by my understanding of human behavior and its relationship to consumer lifestyle trends. In 1995, I established Brenmark House, a marketing think tank for both private and public companies that requires branding, strategic partnerships, joint ventures, licensing and media strategies.

It was during my travels, while helping to build those companies, that I formulated my philosophy for *Tipping for Success*, which not surprisingly holds the same principles as success itself.

WHY I WROTE THIS BOOK

Like the vast majority of books published, *Tipping for Success* was born out of personal experience. People who know me well have always asked, "How do you always get those last-minute table reservations, or a taxicab so fast during rush hour?" Rather than explain, I would just smile. Unlike most social customs, the art of successful tipping comes without instructions. We learn as we go—picking up lessons and pointers from friends, family, and seasoned travelers in the know. Throughout the years, I've developed very specialized methods and principles, and become regarded as an expert in the "art of tipping." In my travels for business and pleasure, I've successfully navigated my way through hundreds of hotels, restaurants and airlines (I have logged well over a million miles), receiving world class service along the way. My experiences and a genuine desire by so many to "know how it is done" led me to write this book and for the first time reveal these secrets. Tipping for Success is for everyone who places a high value on productivity, time and convenience. It was not written to talk about the customary 15 percent tip chart, or answer questions like, "Should a rude waiter be tipped?" It was written to reveal the most important secret for getting "priority attention," that is, not how much to tip, but what to say. This book pulls the curtain back on all those situations where you're short on time and running low on patience!

As a successful entrepreneur, I've learned that the basic principle for tipping effectively is the same principle you need to build a winning business, that is, the ability to connect with people. Though it is brief, you are creating a mutual understanding and expectation between yourself and the other party involved in the tipping mission. This step-by-step guide demystifies the uncertainty of how it is done, so you can move up in line and in your world.

You'll learn 10 of the top secrets such as:

1. How to recognize a tipping opportunity. *(page 17)*

2. What to say when you're told, "Sorry, we're booked." *(page 81)*

3. How to avoid airport lines at baggage check in. *(page 105)*

4. How to become a stealth tipper. *(page 61)*

5. How to identify the key person in charge. *(page 41)*

6. What to do when you're running late and returning a rental car. *(page 118)*

7. How to catch a taxi on a crowded street. *(page 93)*

8. Five ways to pass a tip. *(page 61)*

9. How to strike up a quick rapport. *(page 44)*

10. How to make sure your car is brought up *before* you leave the restaurant. *(page 102)*

As we transition from an analog to a digital world of services, many business travelers wonder what effect the Internet will have on tipping, in terms of getting reservations for those hard-to-get-in places. The Internet, when fully deployed at high data rates with multi-media viewing, will permanently transform the way the majority of people make their reservation and travel arrangements. However, even then and well beyond, there will always be someone responsible for prioritizing the flow of such information. Reading on your screen, "Sorry, we're booked," leaves the patron with the same choices as if hearing it on the telephone. In other words, we're back to what this book is all about, knowing whom to call and what to say.

Throughout *Tipping for Success* you will find this handshake symbol. I've used this symbol because it represents the cornerstone of effective tipping—the relationship. This emblem will highlight some of the more important tips you will want to remember. I offer these tips to you with my compliments. I have been told many times that any one of these secrets alone is worth far more than three times the price of this book.

If you would like to contribute your own experiences, or reveal some great secret(s) you've discovered in your travels, please e-mail them to brennerml@aol.com. Perhaps I can include them in the next edition of *Tipping for Success!*

My very best wishes,

Mark Brenner

The scientific study of the process of social influence has been underway for well over a half a century. Since that time, numerous social scientists have investigated the ways in which one individual can influence another's attitudes and actions. For the past 30 years, I have practiced in that endeavor, concentrating primarily on the major factors that bring about a specific form of behavorial change-compliance with a request. Six basic tendencies of human behavior come into play in generating a positive response: reciprocation, consistency, social validation, liking, authority and scarcity. As these six tendencies help to govern our business dealings, our societal involvements and our personal relationships, knowledge of the rules of persuasion can truly be thought of as empowerment.

Robert B. Cialdini
Author, *Influence*
Regents' Professor of Psychology at Arizona State University
reprinted from *Scientific American* February 2001

Chapter One

TIPPING FOR SUCCESS
— The Right Philosophy

It's easy to make sweeping judgments without having the right perspective. Watching someone move to the front of a line while others are still waiting can appear unfair and really rev up our emotions. Like most aspects of life and business, we live in a competitive world. In school, business, office politics, sports, even finding romance, we are engaged in some sort of competition. Traveling is no different. Whether it's a trip to the supermarket, a weekend getaway or making a simple airport connection, we face long lines and overcrowded aisles. Like it or not, we compete to get the attention we think we deserve. To some who believe that tipping to get priority attention is unfair to those who prefer to wait in their designated long line, I say—the best of luck, I hope your name is called soon. To the rest of us I say—seize your moment!

Every businessperson knows that "time is the enemy of all deals." Every day we are surrounded by situations where the opportunity exists to influence the outcome, positively or negatively, through the *art* of tipping. Tipping has more than made its way into our daily lives here in the United States and abroad. In fact, it's developed its own subculture and language. In New York, it is known as *schmearing* or greasing the wheels, in Chicago they say *seeing the man*, in Las Vegas it is called *toking*, and in Paris they say *pourboire*. Travel to Cairo, they call it *baksheesh*, and in Berlin they say *trinkgeld*. For those who hold my stealth tipping secrets, hearing the phrase "at your service" takes on a whole new meaning.

By applying the techniques and methods in this book, your life as an everyday patron or successful business traveler is about to change. Each day we are surrounded by situations where the opportunity exists to influence the outcome of an anxious moment or an important event, through the *art* of tipping. It seems for many, tipping is often an awkward or embarrassing procedure. It need not be. Knowing what do when faced with the prospect of being "turned away" demands many of the same qualities as getting ahead in life. It requires a sharp instinct and a readiness to act.

To be a successful and confident tipper, you'll need first to understand the context and proper attitude of how to approach and implement the tipping mission. Throughout this book, and particularly in the first few chapters, I emphasize how to apply this new philosophy to help influence a different outcome to an otherwise stressful circumstance. Try not to skip chapters looking for the shortcuts or secrets of what to say or do. Like the magician, secrets alone without an understanding of audience expectation and a well-thought-out presentation will be met with disappointment. *Tipping for Success* is about being prepared. It is as much an attitude as it is a business!

For the business executive focused on the "fast track" to success, saving time is the order of the day. Getting the right person to agree to a meeting is just the beginning. Seasoned business professionals and entrepreneurs know the real fight can be on the battlefield called *travel and entertainment*. It may sound overly simplistic, but sometimes staying at a special hotel because you know certain business contacts are staying there, or getting into a popular restaurant because you know it's a client's favorite, can have a positive influence on achieving a specific goal. I'm not suggesting that your goal wouldn't have been met or a deal wouldn't have closed without having those reservations —that would be an overstatement. I

*Getting a reservation at the **right** place, at the **right** time, can often set the backdrop for the **right** outcome.*

am suggesting that your goal might have been achieved sooner if the arrangements you asked for were available. Getting a reservation at the *right* place, at the *right* time, can often set the backdrop for the *right* outcome.

For the frequent business traveler, saving time is like a sword to the Samurai. Moreover, one of the benefits to be gained from receiving the quality of attention you desire is the increased respect with which you will be regarded as a result of other people's heightened perception of you. These positive perceptions by others can provide new windows of opportunity to trade on. I remember one trip to New York where I had a lunch meeting at the Regency Hotel. Although I was not staying at the hotel, I arrived 30 minutes early to arrange with the maitre d' to be seated at one of those "power tables" in the main dining area. (A power table is a table that is strategically located in the restaurant, giving you a full view

 of the room without compromising your own privacy. Upscale restaurants have only a few such tables.) Anyway, after being seated and while I was having a drink, I spotted a senior executive with a well-known investment banking firm whom I had never met (but wanted to). I noticed him glancing at my table and looking impressed with the kind of attention I was receiving. While I waited for my guest to arrive, I walked over and introduced myself and managed to set an appointment with him for the following day. I really believed that opportunity arose because I was seated at that table. *Tipping For Success* also underscores the importance of chance and luck. Who knows what would have happened had I been seated at a table in the back near the kitchen. Although applied to much weightier issues, I believe that it was Henry Kissinger who once said, "luck favors the prepared."

The methods revealed in *Tipping for Success* apply to a five-star hotel as well as to an all-you-can-eat diner. Somehow, travelers think that if a hotel or restaurant is not rated among the top ten in luxury or popularity, there's less appreciation of quality service and less reason to tip well. Not true. A professional at a popular all-night diner, and a professional at a five-star hotel will both give the same level of service if they are approached and treated the same way.

It is worth repeating that the real secret is knowing not what to tip, but what to say.

Today, the business gurus who teach management skills stress the words "relationship marketing" to enhance and broaden future opportunities. Knowing how to tip for success can accelerate those opportunities, not so much because of the money exchanged, but because of the relationship that has been forged. The art of tipping never assumes the pretentious attitude, "I can buy my way in." People who think that way reveal themselves as arrogant individuals who dismiss another person's dignity, and value people only as a means to an end. Seasoned tippers know this, and maintain their mutual respect, spontaneity and generous spirit.

It is worth repeating that the real secret is knowing not what to tip, but what to say. Your words and attitude must convey confidence and appreciation. These qualities are important in demonstrating that you are worthy of the extra effort and, at the same time, are accustomed to such

"I'm afraid we're booked solid through the holidays, but if you'll give me your address I will send you an application for the second week in January."

personalized service. This style is quite effective and can be surprisingly natural to implement. It will open new doors for those who value being valued.

The secrets for getting in and getting great service are generally thought to be reserved for the wealthy and famous. Not so! A friend of mine, the president of a fortune 500 company, called his favorite hotel for a reservation. He had forgotten there was a convention in town and he couldn't get a room. His status as a wealthy patron was of little value because he didn't know what to say or do after being told, "We're booked solid." Even the finer hotels find themselves reluctantly turning away wealthy patrons!

Chances are you've watched certain men and women traveling through airports, hotels and popular restaurants navigating effortlessly through the stressful maze of crowds and lines. Hearing others being greeted with "Hello, Mr. Roberts, let me carry those things for you," or "Good evening, Ms. Allen, your table is waiting!" can really motivate you to reject the status quo and change your philosophy on tipping. An extra level of service can sure take the edge off a frustrating encounter or an exhausting trip.

It really comes down to this, if you add up at the end of the year how much you've spent on those "extra tips" in order to save time and aggravation, and receive luxury service, you'd see how little it was. Those modest increases provide the most measurable and memorable outcome of events you could imagine. Along with giving joy, tipping has the power to create impressions. More than likely if you receive great service, you'll be back. A graciously given tip can establish your stature and make a powerful lasting impression. A tipping blunder on the other hand can leave you looking ill-mannered, feeling ill-prepared, and disqualify you from the race. So, before you plan your next trip, think about how many service professionals you'll meet along the way that can influence your plans more positively. Be prepared.

Ladies, It's Your Turn!

At the risk of jeopardizing this male franchise, the time has finally come to welcome women to join the club! This marvelous membership has all the advantages and perks men have enjoyed for generations. Believe it or not, according to a great many service professionals in the hospitality industry, the majority of women who travel are either  not comfortable or do not like to push for special accommodations when they're told, "Sorry, we're booked." Well, that's about to change! Soon you'll be hearing phrases like, "your table is waiting," "your reservations are set," or "your car has just been pulled up front with the temperature just right and your favorite CD playing." Ladies, hearing these words will be music to your ears and relief for your feet! Welcome to the club of Tipping for Success.

It's ironic that this whole tipping thing is even an issue when it comes to women. Everyone knows women have an impressive respect for the art of great service. Far more important is their global impact on business and leadership. According to the latest White House National Women's Business Council study completed in 2000, over

9 million women (34 percent of all small businesses) own their own businesses, which generate a combined $3.6 trillion dollars in total sales per year and employ 27 million workers. In addition, and according to Venture One (owned by Reuters), 6 percent of the companies that received venture capital in the year 2000 had women CEOs. Why the majority of women today haven't participated fully in this exchange is really a mystery.

The most frequently asked question regarding the tipping styles between men and women is this: What is the difference between what a man has to do to get "priority service" and what a woman has to do? Surprisingly, there is none! Gender plays very little role from the viewpoint of a service professional in determining the lucky patron to win a great table or land a hard-to-get reservation. Of course, in fairness, there are exceptions. It would be disingenuous of me not to mention that some in charge of the reservation book are still greatly influenced by a woman's unique powers of persuasion.

Having already unlocked the gates of opportunity, and with old stereotypes fading quickly, maitre d's, hotel managers, and, in fact, all service professionals are more than ready to extend every courtesy and extra level of service to women that they offer so easily to men. Truth is, any technique you choose to use for exchanging money, or getting reservations at those "hard to get in places," will not require even one scintilla of change on the part of any woman to do something different from that of a man. So be yourself and be your best!

So the next time you need to be somewhere quickly, remember you're a full member now in the Tipping for Success Club. Use your new secrets with my compliments. Like everything novel that makes our life easier, don't be surprised when you ask yourself, "Wow! Why didn't I do this ten years earlier?"

Chapter Two

THE TIPPING INDUSTRY

Tipping for some people is more annoying than it is satisfying. Many do not want to pay a penny over the normal fare or tab. It's not that they don't want faster service, it's just that they don't want to pay extra for it. Period! Part of what contributes to the notion and attitude that tipping is obnoxious and unfair are those ubiquitous paper cups you see by cash registers after standing in a long line for a morning cup of coffee. It's like having an inexperienced service professional unwittingly appear   to have their hand out.

At the other end of the spectrum, I'm sure you've heard someone express with jealous bitterness that tipping in order to get "priority attention," is out-and-out bribery. Unfortunately, this perspective is more self righteous and judgmental than factual. The difference between the two practices is vast. One is legal and one is not. In matters involving bribery, there are federal and state laws that legislate against such actions, all punishable by heavy fines, jail, license revocations, and so forth. Clearly, there is nothing illegal about tipping a service professional in the private sector for a job well done. While many people resent those who know how to get priority attention, it is nonetheless legal and customary, not to mention fundamental to our economy and culture. This includes a more desirable table at a restaurant or simply not wanting to wait in a long line at an airport curbside check in.

Our entire democratic system is based on free enterprise. In other words, goods and services (except where legislated) go to the highest bidder. Our worldwide system of tipping returns us to a school of fundamental fairness governed by hard work and resourcefulness. It encourages achievement and reward. By definition, the *business* of tipping includes the expectation of *getting* something extra. Some believe it's the "getting something extra" that's not fair to those who expect the same service without tipping. Actually it is quite fair. The same opportunities are available to anyone willing to do more than just accept the status quo. Tipping is not an ethical issue, it's an economic one.

Our worldwide system of tipping encourages achievement and reward.

Each day, millions of individuals and families rely financially on customers to supplement their base salary or hourly wage through tipping. Tipping is important. It lets people know they're reliable and valued. In the context of a competitive and free society we need to better understand this huge segment of our population which takes great pride in providing hospitality to millions of travelers. It's no secret the United States has moved from a manufacturing-based economy to a service-oriented economy. Tipping is here to stay and should be!

If anyone doubts just how important the tipping industry is, consider this:

It has been reported that the U.S. government estimates it will collect over one billion dollars in additional tax revenue each year from the tip income generated from food and beverage employees alone. Total tip income for all tip-related industries, according to one professional estimate, has roughly been forecast to be about

"I regret to inform your lordship that I have been offered, and have accepted an attractive position in valet parking."

$9,000,000,000 a year. According to their figures, that breaks down to about $20,000,000 a day. Tipping is big business. The Federal Tax Equity and Fiscal Responsibility Act (TEFRA) of 1982 was specifically written to insure that the government, too, gets its fair share of this growing industry.

Millions of hard-working people and their families depend on this important supplemental income. Tipping is an accepted and respected part of our free economic marketplace. Hospitality is the world's largest industry, accounting for more jobs, tax revenue and sales than all other areas of commerce. According to current research, the U.S. hospitality industry's employment growth is twice that of any other industry and will become the nation's largest industry by the year 2010.

Chapter Three

I Forgot to Make a Reservation

There are two basic attitudes when sizing up a tipping opportunity.

1. **I have to get these reservations or I'm dead!**
2. **Getting what I need would be nice, but I can live without it!**

In the latter circumstance, other than getting lucky, you probably won't get in. In the event you are successful in getting in, each patron must honestly assess his own predicament, in terms of how much it's worth *before* receiving what he's asking for, and not *after* he gets his result accomplished. This distinction is important because certain patterns of human behavior are predictable. When we really want something, we make all kinds of promises to others and ourselves about how we'll act if it really happens. Then when we get what we wished for, we're sometimes tempted to minimize the importance of what someone did for us to make it happen. Tipping is really no different. For example, forgetting to make reservations in advance and knowing that four people are expecting to meet at a special restaurant will cause you to think to yourself, "If this maitre d' fits me in, boy will I take care of him big time!" That feeling really underscores what this book is all about—the economic value we place on time and convenience.

The Tipping Tolerance Test

To help you better evaluate your own tipping tolerance so you can better determine how willing you are to put your energy into the tipping mission, I've developed The Tipping Tolerance Test. Since you've probably identified yourself as a patron who would like to have a little more skill (and maybe a little more nerve) to shorten those long lines, this test will help evaluate your tolerance threshold for waiting and your willingness to change your attitude toward tipping.

1. *When you show up at a restaurant and are told you have a 30- to 45-minute wait, do you usually wait?*

2. *Are you intimidated if you have to ask a maitre d' or manager, "Can you fit me in earlier?"*

3. *If a hotel or restaurant service person tells you over the phone, "Sorry, we're booked," do you say, "thanks anyway" and hang up?*

4. *Do you resent paying extra for extra service?*

5. *Do you feel self-conscious, as if everyone is watching you, when you ask for special service?*

6. *Do you think tipping is really bribery?*

7. *Do you get angry when you see someone appear from nowhere and get a table or some other service that you've been patiently waiting for?*

8. *Do you feel it's not worth the energy it takes to get the kind of service you want?*

If you've answered YES to one or more of these questions, it means your skills or understanding of the opportunities tipping can provide need improving.

For many people, extra services such as *not waiting* 25 minutes for a table, having their car brought up first, or having a concierge make reservations for an otherwise sold-out engagement, may not hold much value. For others, those same extra services make all the difference in the world! People have different tolerances when it comes to waiting and personal convenience.

Imagine it's 4:00 o'clock in the afternoon, and you just remembered it's your wife's birthday! You have no gift and no plans. Panic sets in! Maybe your marriage has hit a rough spot. Your wife thinks you're going to surprise her tonight by an-nouncing a fabulously planned evening. So far, you've got nothing planned, except begging for forgiveness!! You also know that going to her *favorite* restaurant is the perfect solution. You call the restaurant and are told, "Sorry, we're booked." At that point, you ask yourself, "What's it worth *if* you could get that 7:30 reservation?" My guess is, by that time, the extra few dollars isn't even on your mind!

The same point can be illustrated in another kind of situation. For example, walking downtown in New York City on a bright sunny day looking for a taxi will produce a different kind of urgency than looking for one in a torrential rain storm. With the latter in mind, the question now of how badly you want that taxi becomes an economic issue.

Do Bigger Tips Mean Better Service?

It is not uncommon for many people to think that somehow it takes hundred dollar bills or celebrity status to get great service. I'm not quite sure how this myth came to be, but nothing could be further from the truth! Proof of this fact is that the majority of tips are given after the accommodation has been made. More important factors, such as having the right attitude and developing a natural rapport with a service provider, become the real measures for whether or not you'll achieve your results. One contributing factor for this popular myth (that you have to tip big for better service) is that successful tippers do not, by and large, talk about how they do it! The presumption is: "They must tip BIG!" Successful tippers

think if more people knew "how to do it," then they might be less effective in getting special consideration or priority service. Even friends and family rarely know how they do it. A part of getting great service takes an understanding of mutual respect. There are exceptions! We've all witnessed, from time to time, loud and obnoxious customers who are BIG tippers and are just tolerated. I'm convinced that this type of customer and this kind of behavior are the exceptions and not the rule. Patrons who successfully know how to tip with tact are more thoughtful and have a greater range of people skills.

Hotel managers, maitre d's, concierges, airline supervisors and other service professionals will all attest to the fact that they pay far more attention to how they are spoken to than how much money a customer waves at them. Tipping for success does not require giving lavish amounts of money. Over-tipping can appear vulgar. That's why, before a patron makes his case, he must always show empathy by acknowledging the circumstances a service person is up against, *before* asking for an accommodation.

It is no secret that service professionals generally respond more positively when you acknowledge their perspective and show respect for their authority and circumstances. No one wants to be bullied, threatened, or made to feel "like a circus animal" waiting to perform with a $20.00 bill dangling in front of him. Words like, "Hey, Edward, I'll pay you well. Get me that table," will probably get you nowhere.

By contrast, saying, "Edward, I know you're overbooked tonight and you're really up against it, but if you can make arrangements for a table for three at 8:15 tonight I will really take care of you the right way!" On the

It is no secret that service professionals generally respond more positively when you acknowledge their perspective and show respect for their authority and circumstances.

average, a maitre d' has about three or four opportunities each evening to accommodate last-minute openings. Reasons vary. Sometimes patrons are running late and others call to cancel. Still other times, guests finish their dinner earlier than expected, freeing up another table. Either way, these openings are usually given to those tippers who understood how to communicate respectfully. Maitre d's recognize those customers who truly respect them for what they do for a living. Nothing turns a maitre d' off more than when a customer trivializes his work by thinking, "All they do is walk people to tables!" Like all of us, people feel better about themselves and their jobs when they win the respect and affection of their customers and co-workers. Generally speaking, the turnover for maitre d's at fine restaurants and hotels is very low. These are highly sought after positions and job satisfaction is taken very seriously.

On the average, a maitre d' has about three or four opportunities each evening to accommodate last-minute openings.

Special Holidays

Regardless of how well you apply the methods in this book, there are times when holidays like Christmas and New Year's, or special functions like business conventions and sporting events, become so concentrated within a city that little can be done to get a reservation and influence the outcome. Still, you never want to give up before you try. I'm always amazed how service professionals find a way to accommodate tippers who know the secrets. Proper patience and an understanding of how to complete the tipping mission will substantially increase your likelihood of getting your request met.

Frequent Customer vs. One Time Customer

It's a very comfortable feeling to travel 3,000 miles or even three miles to a favorite spot and be greeted with, "Good evening, Dan. Your table is ready" or "Nice to see you again, Ms. Adams." We all like to be recognized and respected. It makes us feel connected to each other and supports our own personal identity as being a successful person.

One common question that's always asked is: When visiting a new place, and you know you won't be returning, should you tip differently from frequent customers? In a word, No! You never know if you will need some urgent service during your stay. I can remember one time I flew to Chicago for a meeting at the Hyatt Hotel. The meeting was scheduled to last two hours. My first order of business when

I arrived was to introduce myself to the doorman and *Advance Tip* him five dollars. I made a point of telling him I might need his services later. Well, my meeting ran over and had I
not taken care of the doorman earlier that morning, I would not have made my flight. The town was packed from a convention (I had no idea) and there was no time to call for a cab. Billy, the doorman, remembered our talk and immediately flagged down a town car service he does business with for me. I gave him an extra five dollars—an expense far less than the penalty the airline would have charged for a

changed reservation or the financial consequences of not showing up for my next dinner meeting back in Los Angeles.

Another reason to tip the same way (even though you may not ever be back) is to continue carrying the goodwill legacy of the *Tipping for Success* philosophy. I'm sure you've noticed many times when you've been the beneficiary of a kind gesture from a hotel staffer or other service professional for no apparent reason. Such unexpected extra service comes as a result of the standards set from a well-run management team as well the server's individual willingness to work on good faith.

Chapter Four

DRESSING THE PART

Imagine watching a guest standing at a reservations desk wearing a torn sweatshirt and an old pair of sneakers trying to encourage a hotel manager to upgrade his hotel room, or an airline passenger dressed shabbily trying to get a courtesy business class upgrade. Each will more than likely be met with resistance or, worse, refusal. Although the expression "clothes don't make the man" is one of life's truisms, in the case of tipping, "clothes do make the man or woman." The combination of dressing the part and acting the part will oftentimes get you the part! If this seems superficial, then you had better reconsider just how important the special service you are asking for really is. After all, you only get one chance to make a first impression and that usually occurs in the first 30 seconds. The two most important first impressions to a service professional is how you're dressed and how you act!

Unlike casual or social circumstances where someone can take his time in sizing up a person, a service professional must assess a patron's appearance and willingness to reciprocate instantly. So, the next time you're looking for "special

The two most important first impressions to a service professional is how you're dressed and how you act!

consideration," and feel you're being eyed or judged based on what you're wearing, think how, if you were in that position of authority, you might react to someone dressed in a less than desirable way. Would you risk your last reservation?

Naturally there are always exceptions. There have been times when each of us find ourselves looking and feeling like we just got off a 20-hour bus ride but still were able to accomplish our "tipping mission." However, one shouldn't have to count on getting lucky. The idea is to make it as easy as possible and provide more wind to the back of your sail.

With that in mind, it is best to *look the part!*

"Smoking or nonsmoking?"

Chapter Five

GETTING ACCESS

Identify the Person in Charge

Tipping for success requires more than *the risk of being turned down.* The first step to *getting in* is getting access to the key person in charge. Too many times we waste time talking to the wrong person who has no authority. Prior to making your first call to determine who's in charge, think about whom you might know to help get you in. There's much truth to the six degrees of separation theory. You may surprise yourself by realizing you've got some kind of connection through a friend, who has a friend, who knows someone who has access to the person or place you want to get into. Knowing about that connection can really add to your confidence and chances of success. On the other hand, if you don't know anyone and are calling for the first time, simply ask for the name of the person in charge.

There's nothing more frustrating than after 20 minutes of "making your case" realizing the person you are talking to doesn't have the authority to make the decision! Similarly, it's counterproductive when a tipper acts obnoxious and loud, demanding immediate attention from a staff member who simply has no authority. Here are three simple ways to help identify the right person right away.

1. Before you begin discussing your situation with a staff employee, ask (the name and title) of who the supervisor, manager, or maitre d' is in charge.

2. If you are doing this in person and have the extra time, try to listen and watch how that manager is handling other people. It can tell you what kind of authority, attitude and willingness he/she will show you.

3. Take notice of the title on a name badge before you introduce yourself so you can both identify and call that supervisor by name.

Find the Proper Setting

The second step to think about, now that you know who's in charge, will be to decide quickly where the best spot is to have a conversation about your present situation. This part of the tipping process I call — *Stealth Tipping — invisible to the onlooker while achieving your purpose.* The setting you choose to approach the person you're tipping must be considered first, otherwise you might compromise your objective. For example, at a restaurant, do you talk with the

*The first step to **getting in** is getting access to the key person in charge.*

maitre d' at his podium? Do you call him to the side? Remember that everyone can see and hear! Patrons are hungry and tensions run high as customers try to get seated as fast as possible. What about being at a hotel? If the lobby is busy, where is the best place to talk *in private?* Here, too, emotions run high, as most guests are cranky and tired from traveling. Airports pose the same problem. How do you get a ticket agent to leave his or her desk to have your conversation? These are serious considerations if you want to achieve your tipping mission. Each of these questions will be answered in the respective chapters under restaurants, hotels, airports, and so on.

Chapter Six

STRIKING UP A RAPPORT

 Amazingly, striking up a quick rapport can take as little as 15 seconds. Start out by introducing yourself and saying the service person's name first. For example, "Hello, Ms. Herricks, I'm Bob Stevens." Do not begin your conversation with transparent, self-serving compliments or remarks like "How are you tonight?" or "I really like your outfit." These kinds of comments can be taken as insincere. Instead, be direct. Your conversation must have a calm urgency with the promise of a positive result. In some instances you may want to start out by telling the service professional you are in a tough spot. Very tough! You do this because it's empowering and reinforces a professional's desire to help.

The right words said with the right attitude can open more doors than any hundred-dollar bill. As a matter of fact, waving *too* much money in the face of a service professional can be offensive and provoke an uncomfortable feeling. Developing a quick rapport requires creating a positive feeling so that the service professional will want to come through for you. Your communication should inspire confidence, making the service person feel important, capable and worthy. You must know exactly what to say, where to say it, and how long it should take. Looking or sounding unsure and fumbling your words suggest inexperience and sends the message: "I really don't know what I'm doing, so don't waste your favor on me!"

Never, never sound desperate or beg. (That only works in marriage!) To this end, experienced tippers are expected to maintain a successful profile, as well as their humility. It would be self-defeating if the tipper's behavior reflected any impatience or a flared temper. A successful tipping style requires rapport and being discreet. Any behavior marked with arrogance is offensive and would defeat the purpose. Service professionals do not like to be barked at and, as a result, will usually not accommodate such customers.

The right words said with the right attitude can open more doors than any hundred-dollar bill.

It is important to note throughout this book the significant emphasis that is placed on the words *right way.* These two words send a very strong message that you will meet every expectation they have as a service professional. Not the least of which is the right amount of tip. All this encourages your service professional to respond by saying, Yes, I can do that. Come see me!"

Sometimes when you see others do things you wish you could do, you might say to yourself, "That's great for the other guy, but I could never do that." Some people find that just talking with management or anyone in authority is an intimidating process. Honest self-examination may reveal a sort of shyness, rationalization, self-pity or jealousy that can cause people to say to themselves, "Who cares, it's not that important anyway!" What may be more truthful is, either they don't want to put themselves through the process of possible rejection or cannot

Your communication should inspire confidence, making the service person feel important, capable and worthy.

afford the extra money to tip. Tipping for success requires *more attitude* than it does more money! It takes a sustained energy to complete the tipping mission.

Tips to Striking Up a Quick Rapport

1. Address the person by their first name or last name. Then introduce yourself. By saying their name first you establish your respect for their position and authority.

2. Convey your understanding of how difficult it may be to get you that reservation—empathize.

3. Tell a quick compelling story (it may be true or slightly exaggerated) about why you need this accommodation —but don't ramble.

4. Underscore how well you will take care of him/ her. Your words should be sincere and you must sound confident. Your pacing should be deliberate, not rushed.

5. If you are doing this in person, be sure to maintain eye contact.

6. If you are doing this in person, do not smile *too much*. This is serious business. It's not a smiling contest.

Chapter Seven

WHAT TO SAY TO GET IN

Before we examine several different expressions and dialogues to help get you your reservation, I want to draw your attention to the nature of these dialogues. They are very simplistic. They are also direct, to the point and effective. Do not underestimate them. They will work. But only if you say them with the proper emphasis and pacing. If this sounds like you may have to practice in the mirror or with a friend first, you may be right! The truth is, like most communication, it's all in the presentation. When you hear a persuasive point of view, a performer on stage, an actor in a movie, or even a good public speaker, you can judge their effectiveness to the extent you believe or want to believe in what they are saying. Simply said, it feels like an honest moment.

When you're in a tight spot, tipping is serious business. Those in charge of the reservations book are quick to size up a potential tipping patron. Like a good storyteller, you must sound engaging, warm and authentic. It's not important if you think they've heard the same story from someone else.

What is important is for you to convey confidence in what you say. It will take a bit of practice, but it's more than worth it if what you have at stake is really important.

When you hear a persuasive point of view, a performer on stage, an actor in a movie, or even a good public speaker, you can judge their effectiveness to the extent you believe or want to believe in what they are saying.

One more point: Some people might be troubled by telling a made-up story to accomplish a result. Of course, any made-up story is not true. However, saying something that is not true, but does not hurt anyone, is very different from saying something malicious or dishonest that might injure another person. To some degree, most people occasionally say things to one another that are completely untrue. Looking beyond the words for the moment and examining the larger context of that particular relationship, it might be said out of politeness, compassion or practicality. The business of tipping is no different.

Patrons aren't the only ones who try to influence a different outcome to their advantage. Restaurateurs also do this. In my earlier reference to Robert M. Cialdini's article in *Scientific American*, "The Science of Persuasion", he discusses a problem that is common among all restaurateurs—No shows! People who make reservations and simply don't show up. While it is true this is good news for other patrons who walk in last minute, it is unsettling for an owner who has planned a specific number of turns for that table.

To help alter this pattern, a maitre d' or receptionist will need only to change two words of what is said to a caller. By changing from— "Please call if you have to change your reservation," to "Will you please call if you have to change your reservation?" will cause the rate of "no shows" to drop substantially. The pivotal pause after the question was critical in having the patron make the commitment. Even a minor publicly made commitment, according to Professor Cialdini's research in his book, *Influence*, along with a person's need to act consistently with his self image helps direct a person's future actions.

The extra level of service or accommodation you're are about to ask for is what service professionals do for a living.

As patrons, this principle underscores the importance of pausing for a moment after asking a maitre d', "Robert, will you be able to make those arrangements?"

Remember, the extra level of service or accommodation you're about to ask for is what service professionals do for a living. So don't feel embarrassed. If you're feeling tense about being on the spot and not having the reservation you need, don't show it. Be engaging and to the point. Try to remember, most of what you'll be asking for is "business as usual" for the person in charge.

With all this in mind, here are some suggestions and variations on a theme that will establish your credibility quickly when calling for reservations. Although at first it may feel unnatural to use such expressions, remember your goal is to achieve a positive response from the service professional. By all means, adapt these expressions to your own personality, but do not stray too far from the spirit or focus of your mission.

1. *"Hello Robert, my name is Brad Thompson. Bob Meyers suggested that I call you if I was in a tight spot—I am. Perhaps you can help. Sorry for the last minute call, but I would be happy to take care of you the right way if you can make arrangements for a table of four tonight at 7:15. I will be very happy to show you my appreciation when I arrive."*

By saying you're from New York or used to work in New York, you have instant credibility as a person who values time and convenience.

2. *"Hello Robert, my name is Brad Thompson. I'm from New York and I'm in a spot. I have some important guests with me tonight and would be very grateful if you could squeeze in a 7:30 dinner reservation tonight for three. Robert, I will really make it worth your while—BIG time. Can you make those arrangements?"*

3. *"Hello Robert, my name is Brad Thompson and I've just arrived from New York. I'm in a difficult situation and was told you might be able to help me. I realize many new*

customers make promises they don't keep, but I can assure you, I will more than make it worth your time if you will make arrangements tonight for a party of four at 7:30. I promise, you will remember this reservation as one of your favorites! Thank you."

(Note- If this seems dramatic, it is. This approach is suggested when you are being met with resistance as a new customer and feel you are getting nowhere.)

4. *"Hello Robert, I am calling on behalf of Mr. Brad Thompson. He is arriving this afternoon at the airport at 5:00. I know this is last minute, but Mr. Thompson has assured me he will take care of you the right way—if you can fit in his party of four in tonight at 7:30. Can you make those arrangements?"*

One final suggestion: If everything you're saying to a maitre d' appears futile and you're still being told, "I'm sorry, there's nothing I can do," immediately suggest that you don't mind waiting in the bar area, if that will help. This sends a strong signal that you're reasonable in terms of how long you're willing to wait. It takes pressure off the maitre d' to know you're not a nagging patron. However, should the maitre d' take you up on your suggestion, be prepared when you arrive to greet him using both the Advance Tip Method *(page 54)* and the Double Handshake *(page 65)*. Say something like, "Good evening, Edward, I'm Mr. Thompson and I wanted to let you know how much I appreciate your helping me out tonight." At that point, he will likely remind you to wait a short while in the bar area. Don't be surprised if he offers to buy a round of drinks for you and your guests while waiting.

Why It Helps to Say, "I'm from New York."

Although not everyone likes New Yorkers, they do (as a rule) have a reputation of knowing how to get things done! They are also known as people of action! With over 8 million people in the city, speed and efficiency are highly rewarded and regarded. By saying you are from New York or used to work in New York, you have instant credibility as a person who values time and convenience.

Chapter Eight

TIPPING THREE WAYS

– Advance, After Service, The Tip Gift

The Advance Tip is the most effective method for assuring results. It has an immediate overtone that suggests: "I mean business." More importantly, it conveys the message, "I won't waste your time, please don't waste mine!" This strategy will insure that you'll be taken care of with the highest degree of consideration.

It's interesting to note that the origins of tipping began in the 1800's with patrons using the Advance Tip Method. It was with the expectation of getting "fast" service that the acronym TIP, (To Insure Promptitude) became the motivating factor for tipping in advance of the service. Later, as tipping became more commonplace, customers generally began tipping *after* receiving service.

In contrast to after service tipping, service professionals know there are always a few customers who promise more, but in the end give less. With advance tipping, there can be no mistake. It also demonstrates that the tipper has tremendous confidence in the service professional's ability to comply. It's a sign of respect and competence for the service professional. Advance Tipping also establishes the relationship more quickly and defines the job at hand. However, it is not foolproof. Although reasons may vary, there is a chance your service professional just can't get the job done to your satisfaction (although he or she will still try). The Advance Tip is the closest thing to a sure thing.

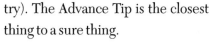

The Advance Tip is the most effective method for assuring results.

If you're not a regular customer and the service person does not know you, tipping in advance could carry several small risks. First, if the amount you're tipping in advance is not enough, you may unwittingly forfeit the end result of what you wanted. For example, giving a maitre d' five dollars at a very high-end restaurant that is overbooked may result in no table at all. Secondly, if he does accept the five dollars, you may now have to wait longer than you expected or at the very least, wind up with a poor table   by the kitchen. So always think twice about what you really think is fair, in relation to how crowded the place is and how important *getting in* is to you.

Advance tipping also carries the small risk that a well-meaning manager or maitre d' may not meet your expectation. On very rare occasions, where I have tipped in advance and not received the promised service, I have seen the tip returned. Ordinarily, service professionals will honor this code of performance. Service professionals in general will not accept money unless they feel they can perform and satisfy. When using the Advance Tip strategy, the Double Handshake Method *(page 71)* is recommended for passing the tip. It rarely fails to secure the right response, since it conveys all the right messages and leaves no doubt about your intentions.

The Advance Tip is the closest thing to a sure thing.

One final point: As a general rule, the hotel concierge is one service professional who prefers NOT being tipped in advance. A concierge takes great pride in being able to provide world class service for their guests without any advance incentives. Only after completing the service(s) for a guest, does a concierge feel most comfortable in accepting a gratuity for a job well done. The concierges at the finer hotels and resorts generally prefer this tipping etiquette. *(See Hotels, Chapter Eleven)*

After Service Tip

The After Service Tip remains the most popular with patrons. Service professionals know this and have come to rely on the "good faith" of each customer to fulfill the promise of gratitude. The After Service Tip strategy is typically used with the Single Handshake Method *(page 64)* when it is time to express appreciation.

The Tip Gift

The most under utilized form of tipping (other than during the holiday season), is the Tip Gift. If you're looking to build goodwill and forge a stronger relationship with any service

There are times when giving a standard money tip can be taken as an insult.

professional, there's no more convincing way to show your gratitude than this kind of tip. The idea of sending a thank you card or gift after having received world class service will be taken as the ultimate sign of respect and appreciation. This important tip expression can be given either in person or by mail. In those instances where you are a new customer and planning to return with great frequency, the tip gift makes a great "first day" impression. Try it once and the next time you need a priority reservation, there will be little doubt of getting it! If you're wondering what kind of gift to give, make it thoughtful but not too personal. For example it would be inappropriate to give cologne or perfume. A more appropriate gift would be a gift certificate, bottle of wine, or a gift basket.

You probably know that every so often a relationship between a patron and a service professional grows to become more personal. There are times when giving a standard money tip can be taken as an insult. I remember one incident where my wife and I had a terrible argument at one of our favorite restaurants and she left the table visibly upset. The maitre d' who had known us for more than five years extended himself and offered her an understanding ear. After about five minutes, she returned with a little smile and a feeling of well being. I appreciated the maitre d's input and upon leaving tried to give him ten dollars. There was no question he felt offended. I immediately realized why. By giving a money tip I diminished and trivialized his genuine caring by looking as though I was paying him for his concern. I had minimized "our relationship," which sent the signal *you only care when I pay you*. A better solution would have been to send a Tip Gift such as a nicely gift-wrapped sport shirt, or a dozen golf balls with a card that read: "Frank, thanks for the other night." Even a handshake after dinner showing genuine appreciation would have sufficed. Sometimes money is just not the right way to say thank you.

Chapter Nine

FIVE METHODS FOR PASSING A TIP

Perhaps second in importance to knowing what to say is *how to pass the tip!* Like the art of close-up magic, the skill of tipping discreetly and appearing natural while concealing the surprise must be practiced. Folding and passing the money is no different! In the case of tipping, I call this art form *stealth tipping.* In other words, appearing below the radar of everyone's watchful eye. With the exception of a few different kinds of circumstances, no one should ever see how or when you pass the tip. It's considered in bad taste to take money out in full view, counting and folding while everyone watches. Choosing the right method to pass the tip is critical in helping to shield the tipper (as well as the service provider) from any possible embarrassment or confrontation with other patrons who may have been waiting longer. Being a *stealth* tipper also includes, to the extent that it's possible, having a conversation that no other patron suspects or hears. I have identified several *stealth* tipping techniques in the following chapters. They are sure to keep your maneuvers anonymous. So, be prepared, know your plan and look relaxed as you approach the service professional.

4 Quick Don'ts:

Choosing the right method to pass the tip is critical in helping to shield the tipper (as well as the service provider) from any possible embarrassment or confrontation with other patrons who may have been waiting longer.

1. With the exception of valet parking, bellmen, skycaps, hailing a cab, or other accepted public tipping situations, never take money out from your pocket or purse and wave it in full view for everyone to see. It's garish and offensive. Think stealth and remain prepared with money folded in your palm.

2. If you decide to use the Advance Tip Method, always introduce yourself first, striking up a quick rapport, *before* you place money in someone's hand. It takes only a few seconds. I have seen many people try this the other way, only to be rejected. It shows the service professional a certain degree of disrespect and negates their powers of discretion. It's like saying you'll do anything for money, without even knowing what it's for!

3. Another potentially offensive method of tipping, which has been popularized by some movies, is the tearing in

half a large bill ($20 $50 $100) and promising a maitre d'
or waiter he will get the other half upon completing a service. With few exceptions (such as asking a taxi driver to
"wait"), it is taken as demeaning to one's self respect and
independence. It's like saying, "Be a good boy, do what I say
and you can have this!" This is a big turn off.

4. One more final practice that should be discouraged: The
   placing of folded money, without permission, in someone's
   top pocket, pants pocket, etc. This invasion of a person's personal space is universally regarded as the *most offensive.*

Regardless of the technique you select, or the circumstance
you find yourself in, remind yourself to relax. You're not com-
mitting a crime and you won't be making any getaways! Your
manner should be casual and relaxed. I suggest practicing first
with a friend. Within a few short minutes you will begin to feel
comfortable and confident. Remember that these methods are
effective only in conjunction with the right attitude and the
warm rapport you create. When tipping more than ten dollars,
try not to use too many singles. Having too many bills in your
hand makes for a bulkier and more cumbersome feel when
exchanging money.

1. Single Handshake

Of all the tipping methods, this one is the most natural. It utilizes the universal handshake, which has the built-in surety of the "no tell" tip off. In places where many eyes may be watching, the Single Handshake is undetectable.

The Technique:

1. Fold the bill(s) in half.

2. Fold bill(s) in half again.

3. Turn the bill(s) horizontally and place it on the inside of your right palm with the corner edge of the bill, on the first crease of the 3rd and 4th fingers of your right hand. Keep your hand naturally cupped so the bill is concealed in the palm of your hand. Look directly into the eyes of the receiver as you casually offer your right hand to shake his, leaving the folded bill(s) inside the receiver's palm.

2. Double Handshake

This style of handshaking is used when you want to convey a real warmth and appreciation for the courtesy being shown to you. It has strong overtones, which suggest that the tip in your hand is more than the usual amount and emphasizes the importance of your request. When you practice this, you will instantly feel the emotional and physical connection between you and the receiver. This method grew out of years of observing how people greet each other when they genuinely want to convey deep appreciation and sincerity.

The Technique:

1. Fold the bill(s) in half.

2. Fold bill(s) in half again.

3. Turn horizontal & place inside the right palm.

4. Extend right hand with folded bill concealed as the tippers left hand is placed on the outside of the service professionals right hand.

This starts out exactly the same way as the Single Handshake with the exception that as both parties shakehands the tipper immediately and firmly places his left hand on the top side of the service person's hand. Remember, the folded bill(s) is now inside the tipper's right hand, ready for the hand off.

3. Peel Method

This is the exception to the rule, *never tip in full view*. For valet parking attendants, ushers, stadium or other outdoor service professionals, this category of profession-

al is generally comfortable receiving visible tips. They actually prefer it as it serves as a reminder to other people watching, "Hey, it's okay to take care of me."

The Technique:

1. *Right hand holds handful of folded bills.*

2. *Left hand opens the folded bills and peels back completely one bill at a time.*

3. *Left hand folds remaining bills back in half again and passes them to the service professional.*

It is best to use multiple dollar bills folded in half and held in the left hand as the right hand peels off one bill at a time. It is counted in full view for the attendant to see. You can show a little flair with this method.

4. Agent Method

If ever there were an inventive method for getting priority attention, it would be the Agent Method. It has unlimited applications. Whether at a hotel, valet parking, coat room or, of course, a restaurant, this method employs the help of a second party who handles the transaction on behalf of the tipper. In the case of restaurants, the tipper instructs and enlists a second person (usually the one he or she is with) to speak to the maitre d' on his or her behalf. It helps create a mystique of authority. Most professionals think (and rightfully so) that people who employ others on their behalf to arrange for the daily details of life are very successful. It is impressive and sets up the expectation that you are used to results. It also works on another level. Service professionals respond positively because the person making the offer is also employed, and thus encourages camaraderie. *It's pure stealth.*

The Technique:

1. *Fold the bill(s) in half.*

2. *Fold bill(s) in half again.*

3. *Turn horizontal & place inside the right palm.*

4. *Extend right hand with folded bill(s) concealed. This method can utilize either the single or double handshake.*

5. Signal Method

Once you have the person's attention, the bills you have in your hand do not necessarily have to coincide with what you tip. The sole objective is to catch their attention! This is very effective when hailing a taxi on a crowded street or catching the attention of a food or souvenir vendor at an event.

The Technique:

Bills are fanned out in one hand held above the head.

With a handful of fanned out dollar bills held above your head, one hand is casually waived in the air to catch the attention of the person you want. For taxis, depending on the direction you are going, the right hand is suggested because it is closest to the street and easier for the driver to see.

Chapter Ten

Restaurants
— *Getting a Table*

 There are three objectives when calling for a reservation. First, getting the reservation. Second, getting the right time so you don't wind up eating dinner at 10pm or lunch at 3:30, and third, getting the right table.

Later I'll discuss the actual dialogues used to get you your reservation. However, do not underestimate the importance of getting the right time slot especially if you want to catch a movie, visit friends or be somewhere else at a certain time.

If seating is important to you, you'll also want to know what to say rather than be surprised when you are seated near the kitchen or next to the busing station. Never make the mistake of thinking that if you get your reservation you're set. Keep in mind, expensive restaurants also have cheap seats! Many fine restaurants have different room themes ranging from the quiet and subdued to the "action" packed, filled with people who like to be seen and heard. Let the maitre d' know which room you prefer by saying something like, "Edward, I would prefer the main dining room," or "I'll need a quiet table. I have some important guests with me tonight."

The significance of being seated at the right table is certainly not new. During the grand old days of Hollywood, stars like Bogart, Garbo, Dietrich, Marx Brothers, Sinatra, Astaire, and even Ronald Reagan and Henry Kissinger brought new meaning to the power table concept. At that time, there were less than half a dozen restaurants where the luminaries hobnobbed. Many of the most well-known celebrities, their agents and studio heads made it a point to be seated at the best tables. In some cases, *the* best table! Great service and spectacular food was expected. The real prize was the right seating. In his last unfinished book, *Answered Prayers*, Truman Capote captured that sentiment when he wrote:

"A table in Siberia, please."

> *Preferred clients, selected by the proprietor with unerring snobbism, were placed in the banquette-lined entrance area —a practice pursued by every restaurant of established chic. These tables, always nearest the door, are drafty, afford the least privacy, but nevertheless, to be seated at one, or not, is a status-sensitive citizen's moment of truth.*

A Word about Getting Great Service

Now that you've got your table, and assuming you may require an extra level of service during your lunch or dinner, you will again be faced with explain- ing to the waiter what kind of service you're expecting. This conversation can be avoided. Since you've already persuaded the maitre d' to give you a table in the first place, tell him again the kind of service you would like and ask him to mention it to the waiter or waitress on your behalf. I can assure you this will carry more weight and

Keep in mind, expensive restaurants also have cheap seats!

prestige than if you asked yourself. Waiters will pay even more attention to you if they know their own management is tracking them. It also saves you the energy of another con- versation. This strategy is very effective. Since you've already left your maitre d' with a good impression and tip, you can bet that he or she will gladly make a few trips back to your table making sure that everything is to your satisfac- tion. If you're entertaining clients, this kind of attention is very impressive.

As an added touch, when the people you are with are really important to you, tell the maitre d' (in your earlier conversation) that you'd like to have the chef come out and talk about some special entreé or ask about the way one of your guests would   like his or her dish prepared. This never fails to get the appetite going, as well as the imagination of your guest(s) who will wonder how often you may dine

71

there and how important you may be! If this kind of attention seems over the top or too extravagant, it is! However, it's also flattering. At the right time and for the right guest(s), this goes over BIG.

Car Check Technique

An Added Time Saving Jewel

Here's a great time saving idea that allows your waiter to provide a different kind of service. I call it the Car Check

Technique. Here's how it works. When your waiter brings the check, hand him your valet ticket stub and ask, "Would you please be so kind to give this to the valet attendant outside. I'm in a bit of a hurry tonight." Tell him this with confidence, but *not* arrogantly. You want him to get the feeling you've done this many times. At first your waiter may be surprised at such an unusual request, but very quickly you will see a genuine willingness to accommodate. The reason is quite simple. The timing of asking him to do this will be at the same time you are reviewing your bill and adding the tip. Your waiter will be very aware of this. Don't worry if somehow you are unable to coordinate this timing. Chances are he will still do it, as long as you've treated him respectfully throughout his service.

The obvious reason to ask at the time you're finalizing your bill is that in another few minutes you'll be getting up and putting on your coat to leave. In those five minutes, until you make your way out of the restaurant, he will have already handed the attendant your parking stub so your car will be in front. The result: No waiting and no hassles! This is a real jewel of a service and one of the best-kept secrets for those in the know!

Having your waiter do this does not require an extra tip. Getting great service does not require a follow-up tip on every request. Be generous once and it will go a long way. If part of this method sounds familiar, it's another application of the perspicacious Agent Method. *(page 67)* Use this strategy wisely at hotels or anywhere you want to be more anonymous.

Coat Rooms

This is one of those small opportunities even an experienced tipper can sometimes overlook. It makes no difference if the coat room is in a restaurant, museum, convention, hotel, or other establishment. The routine is the same. Take a ticket and park your coat, bag, briefcase, umbrella, packages, whatever. No big deal when you arrive (except if it's raining). The real tension takes place when you leave. This little corner can become a madhouse. I've seen long lines with as many as fifty people.

This can be avoided. Of course, if it's a small event or restaurant you won't have to worry. Otherwise, when you check in, use the Advance Tip Method and tell the coat check person, discreetly (while you're leaning forward), "Hello, my name is Mr. Brenner. I'm going to be needing your help a little later when I leave." (At this point, extend your hand and employ the Advance Tip Method using the Single Handshake.) Continue saying, "I will be sending someone from your staff to see you with my ticket and would like you to hand him my coat immediately. Please leave my coat in front so there won't be any delay. I'll be back in about an hour and a half. Will you take care of this for me?" Rarely will this approach fail. Five dollars, a pleasant smile and a thank you will work just fine.

Maitre d's feel flattered when you remember their names (and slightly embarrassed when they forget yours). It sends the message you've been there before.

One of the most obvious reasons for having a staff member do this for you is to avoid any confrontation with those other patrons *(who have not read this book)* who are still waiting in line after 25 minutes. This *stealth technique* will deliver your private belongings pronto. Naturally you will have to tip the second staffer for performing this service. Three or four dollars will suffice. Be sure to stand discreetly out of the way so you can be on your way!

Find the Proper Setting to Pass the Tip

For the host, hostess or maitre d', the podium is considered their office. Try to keep in mind that everyone can see and hear. Customers are hungry and the atmosphere may be tense as people try to get seated as fast as possible. When you catch his attention, work calmly but quickly. Upon arrival, and assuming you have your reservation already, introduce yourself to the maitre d' and thank him for making the arrangements. As he is walking you to your table, use the Single Handshake Method.

The Halfway Method

When too many eyes are looking and his podium is being leaned on like an information booth at Grand Central Station, try the Halfway Method. Here's how this *stealth* method works:

When you see that the maitre d' has just finished seating another table, walk directly toward that table and meet him halfway in the restaurant aisle. This is where you present your case!

When you see that the maitre d' has just finished seating another table, walk directly toward that table and meet him halfway in the restaurant aisle. This is where you present your case! While it is true you may feel like all eyes are on you, they actually are not. Waiters and waitresses are busy working to keep their customers satisfied. Likewise, patrons who are seated could care less about other customers who are still waiting in the frenzy.

Four Restaurant Reservation Methods

1. Telephone

First, find out the name of the person in charge of handling reservations. There are several ways to do this. Call and ask,

"Who's on tonight taking reservations?" If the person that answers the phone replies, "I am," *immediately* ask, "Who's this please?" (politely and inquisitively). After they tell you their name, say, "Oh Tom, I didn't recognize your voice," then go into your pitch. If the person who answers the phone isn't in charge, ask who is. When that person gets on the phone, immediately start from a place of familiarity by using their first name. The maitre d' seats hundreds of people each month. Maitre d's feel flattered when you remember their names (and slightly embarrassed when they forget yours). It sends the message you've been there before. It also helps create an additional willingness to oblige and accommodate.

The following dialogues and strategies are recommended when you know the restaurant is really jammed up. Try to maintain a certain degree of formality in your conversation without sounding too stiff or rigid. You want to give the impression you have done this many times before.

Suggested Telephone Conversation #1

Tipper: *Good afternoon/evening, Edward. This is Mr. Gordon. Would you please make arrangements for a table for four at the 8:00pm seating tonight. Thank you.*

Maitre d': *I'm sorry, we're booked up!*

Tipper: *I understand. I have just arrived today from New York and would be very happy to take care of you properly if you could find your way to make those arrangements?*

Maitre d': *Well, Mr. Gordon, I might be able to seat you at 8:30. Will that be acceptable?*

Tipper: *That'll be fine. Thank you, Edward. See you tonight.*

As you can see, this call was met with very little resistance. Lets look at another dialogue where the customer must overcome even more resistance.

Suggested Telephone Conversation #2

Tipper: *Good afternoon/evening, Edward. This is Mr. Gordon. Would you please make arrangements for a table of four at 8:00pm this evening. Thank you.*

Maitre d': *I'm sorry, we're booked up. I can give you a 6:30 or a 9:45 reservation.*

Tipper: *I understand. Unfortunately that won't work. I have just arrived today from New York. Eddie, I know how busy you are tonight with the convention in town and I will be very happy to take care of you the right way if you could find your way to make those arrangements for 8:00?*

Maitre d': *There's nothing I can do.*

Tipper: *Edward, let me again emphasize that I will be happy to take care of you generously if you could find a way to squeeze an 8 pm reserva tion in. I understand I may have to wait. That's okay. Do you think you can try to make that happen? I will really make it worth your while.*

Maitre d': *Mr. Gordon, come in at 8 o'clock and see me.*

2. Last Minute Walk-In

Whenever possible, prior to walking in at the last minute, first find out the name of the maitre d' or host who will be in charge of the reservation book. (You can ask a waiter or busboy.) Approach the maitre d' directly *(See Chapters Six and Nine)* and use both the Advance Tip and Double Handshake Methods while delivering the following suggested dialogue:

Tipper: *Good evening, Edward. Bob Gordon. I know you're really backed up now. Normally I would have called last week but my travel plans got changed. Could you arrange for a party of four tonight at 8:00? (Begin Advance Tip Method, using the Double Handshake Method.) Perhaps you could take a second look at your roster. I would be very grateful."*

Maitre d': *Well, Mr. Gordon, I might be able to seat you at 8:15. Will that be acceptable?"*

Tipper: *"That will be fine. Thank you, Edward.*

3. Advance Walk-in

Here's a real gem of a method if you know in the morning or afternoon you need a dinner reservation for the same evening. Remember, get the maitre d's name first before arriving. Most maitre d's arrive at work mid-morning. By walking in mid-morning or late afternoon and introducing yourself, you'll have the time and privacy to make a real impression and ask for your favor. It also underscores how important this must be to you. True, you'll have to go out of your way a bit to drive there, but if that particular restaurant is a place you've got to get into, it's worth it.

Tipper: *Hello, Edward. I'm Bob Gordon. I know you are expecting a full house tonight. I came in especially early as this occasion is very impor tant. I will be very happy to take care of you the right way if you could please make arrangements for a table for four at 8:00 tonight. You won't be disappointed.*

Maitre d': *I'm sorry we're booked up!*

Tipper: *I understand. You can see I drove a consider able distance to see you. Normally I would have called last week but my travel plans got changed. (Begin Advance Tip Method placing $20 in his palm.) Perhaps you could take a second look at your roster. I would be very grateful.*

Maitre d': *Well Mr. Gordon, I might be able to seat you at 8:15. Will that be acceptable?*

Tipper: *That will be fine. Thank you.*

4. Phone Booth Method

This is one of my favorite *stealth* methods. Once you're in the restaurant and you see the difficulty in talking privately with the host or maitre d', go to the nearest telephone booth (or use your cell phone) and ask for the maitre d' by name. This impressive technique will reveal your *unique resourcefulness.* When he gets on the phone, begin the following dialogue:

Tipper: *Hello, Eric, this is Fred Robertson. I'm in your restaurant now and did not want to embarrass you as you have so many people standing at your desk. I would be very happy to take care of you the right way if you could manage to arrange for a table for four at 7:15. I know you are jam packed tonight but I will really make it right for you. In a few minutes I can introduce myself to you at your front desk so as not to cause any disruption. Again my name is Fred. Robertson. Can we work together on this?*

Maitre d':   *Absolutely. Please see me.*

Chapter Eleven

HOTELS

— *Getting a Room Reservation*

Before we go into the details of what to say and do when you've been told, "Sorry, we're booked up," here are two quick suggestions to think about before you place your call for a reservation.

First, give some thought as to where you would like the location of your room. Nothing is more disappointing than to find out after you arrive that your room is next to the ice machine, or worse yet, a fifteen-minute walk to the main lobby.

Second, be specific in asking for a room that's convenient regarding your needs. If you're doing business you may need a fax machine or a separate sitting area for meetings or, if you're celebrating an anniversary or desire some special atmosphere, a city or ocean view may be just the ticket! Just as getting the right table at a restaurant can be important, staying in the right room can make all the difference in the world. In our rush to make travel arrangements and get confirmed, it's easy to forget our real travel objectives.

Find the Proper Setting to Pass the Tip

When it comes to hotel tipping, your conduct above all should reflect the ambience and character of the hotel's environment. Assuming the hotel lobby is bustling with guests and the General, Assistant or Reservation Manager is on his or her way to meet you, scan the hotel lobby in advance to locate a more private area, such as a corridor or corner spot to have your initial conversation.

The Corridor Technique

This *stealth* technique works great when guests or co-workers surround the person you want to speak with. No matter how large or intimate a hotel may be, finding a small corridor to talk privately is relatively easy. Try not to start your conversation in the middle of the lobby! Most guests are a little edgy as people are trying to check in and check out as fast as possible. As you introduce yourself, hand him your business card (assuming it has some look of importance,) saying something like, "Hello, Mr. Stratford, I'm Mark Brenner. Can we talk privately for a moment, thank you?" This will also create a little dramatic tension that will work in your favor. Initially, the manager will not know what it is about.

How Much to Tip

That's always the remaining question. If you are fortunate enough to win a reservation knowing the hotel is overbooked because of a holiday, special weather conditions or an important convention, you'll want to show your appreciation more generously. Still not sure how much to tip? Ask yourself this key question: How important to you is getting that reservation? If you are unsuccessful in finding a comparable hotel room elsewhere, you will feel that the extra tip you had in mind would have been a bargain! More importantly, you will have established a key relationship, which means, next time you won't have to scramble at the last minute.

Getting A Lower Room Rate

If you've achieved a confirmed reservation after knowing the hotel you're staying at is overbooked, bargaining for a better rate at that moment is not wise. However, there is a strategy you can use upon arrival that will usually help in getting a lower rate. Prior to arriving in town, it is wise to know the names of the larger corporations who do business with the particular hotel you want to stay at. To a large extent, most of the larger companies use a majority of the same hotels in the area for out-of-town employees, business associates, seminar functions and salespeople when they are visiting. For example, it's no secret that Los Angeles is home to the entertainment industry. Disney, Warner Brothers, Time Warner, ABC, NBC and CBS all have tremendous name influence with the majority of hotels. In New York, it might be the financial companies like Salomon Smith Barney, American Express, Bank of America, or Lehman Brothers—you get the idea.

Upon arrival, do not discuss your situation with any of the on-duty registration clerks. Ask for the reservations manager or assistant reservations manager. If you're in town trying to do business with a high profile company, you don't have to stand on pride and pay the hotels full price. After introducing yourself, hand your business card to the person you're talking with and mention the company you're seeing in town. Let the reservations manager know your objective by saying: "Hello, Ms. Evans, I'm Mark Brenner. Perhaps you can help. I've just arrived in town for meetings with CBS, and the studio recommended I stay at the Universal Hilton (name their hotel). I was told I would receive their corporate rate. I usually stay at the Sheraton Universal (name the competitor) and only pay $190. "When my secretary made the reservations and she informed me of the $325.00 rate, I instructed her to accept it, knowing I would be able to talk with you personally when I arrived." Follow up that statement with, "I do a lot of business with CBS, as do my associates, and would be grateful if you would make an adjustment on the rate."

I cannot emphasize enough the proper demeanor you must maintain to achieve the results you're looking for. In these few moments, I can assure you, the reservations manager will be sizing you up as a potential "player." Maintaining your confidence is essential.

Naturally there are times when a hotel simply has no rooms. For those times, here's a little-known reservation secret when everything you try and say to get a room is in vain. Many times there are just no rooms available. As a rule, confirmed reservations are held until 6:00pm. Many hotels will release those rooms that were previously reserved and sell it to the next guest who calls after 6:00pm. When all other reservation methods fail, ask about that policy.

Three Hotel Reservation Methods

1. Telephone

When you're being met with resistance, ask for the general manager, assistant general manager or reservations manager. It's a good idea to find out their names prior to getting one of them on the phone. Unlike restaurants, where most people are more informal and don't mind being called by their first name, the hotel business is a lot more formal. It is recommended that you address a key manager by his or her surname, such as Mr. Olson or Ms. Cooper. This sets a professional tone right from the start and positions you as a seasoned traveler. It also distinguishes you from most other guests who become overly familiar too soon. If the hotel is oversold, let the reservations manager know that you realize he or she is up against tremendous pressure. Tell the person that you will be happy to take care of them in a big way and the right way if they can somehow free up one room. At this time, don't ask for a special room or a bigger suite. The object is to get in. Keep your eye on the ball and the tipping mission at hand!

Telephone Conversation #1

Tipper: *Hello, Ms. Graham. This is Mr. Gordon.*

Reservations
Manager: *May I help you?*

Tipper:	*I know you are oversold tonight. I have stayed at your hotel for many years. I am more than happy to really make it worth your while if you could reserve a room for me.*
Reservations Manager:	*Unfortunately, we're sold out.*
Tipper:	*Ms. Graham, I know how difficult this is. We are both business people and I will really make it right in a big way. I am in a spot and really need your help.*
Reservations Manager:	*Please see me upon your arrival.*
Tipper:	*Thank you, Ms. Graham.*

2. Walk-In Hotel Reservation

Tipper:	*Hello, Ms. Graham. Can I have a word with you privately?*
Reservations Manager:	*Sure.*
Tipper:	*Ms. Graham, I know how crowded your hotel is now and how hard your staff is working. (At this point, begin the Double Handshake Method.) I would be very grateful if you could find a way to reserve a room. If it will make it easier for you I can wait till after 6 pm.*
Reservations Manager:	*I believe we can work something out.*

3. House Phone Method

Like the Phone Booth Method used for getting a restaurant reservation, the House Phone Method works virtually the same way. If you've spotted the reservations or hotel manager, but are unable to get his or her attention because guests or staff surround him, go to the nearest house phone and ask for the person by name. When you get the person on the phone, let him or her know that you didn't want to embarrass them by talking in front of the guests or co-workers, and begin the following dialogue.

Tipper:	*Hello, Ms. Graham, this is Fred Robertson, I am in your hotel now and did not want to interrupt you with so many people standing around you. I know you're booked solid, but I would be very happy to take care of you the right way and in a big way if you could manage to reserve a room for me. I know how hard you and your staff are working right now to accommodate your guests. I really will make it right for you. Again my name is Mr. Robertson. Can we work together on this?*
Reservations Manager:	*Absolutely. Please see me at the front desk in about five minutes.*

Valet Hotel Parking

If you've rented a car and find yourself having to leave it with the hotel's valet parking service, here's another great time saving idea. Before leaving your room, call the front desk or ask to be connected to valet parking. Tell the person you're in a bit of a hurry (giving your ticket number), and would appreciate if he would arrange for your car to be brought up now. Be sure to underscore that you are in a hurry, otherwise you may have to wait longer than you want. By the time you leave your room and your elevator arrives, your car will be on the way and waiting for you outside. It doesn't get any easier. And, the tip you give the doorman would have been the same anyway had you not called ahead in the first place. Sometimes when I check in, I introduce myself to the valet manager leaving behind a crisp ten dollar bill and letting him know I prefer my car to be left upfront all the time.

Hotel Ready Team

Here are some other hotel professionals and the services they perform to make your stay more comfortable and more memorable.

The Hotel Manager

This is the man or woman who can make just about anything happen! Carry his or her name and direct dial number just like you carry your American Express card, in the event any part of your stay should go awry. The mere mention of the hotel manager's name to other hotel employees can assure you of special accommodations. If you want to take out *special insurance* with respect to anticipated problems, he's your man. After you check in, even though you may require no immediate special services, you would be wise to make your introduction and leave behind a good impression as to what you may need during your stay. The hotel manager will take this "heads up" as an indication of the caliber of service you're used to.

The Concierge

In French it means *Keeper of the Keys,* as a guest it will mean a gracious host. The concierge has been empowered by management to help make each guest's stay more relaxed and comfortable. Upon arrival, if there is a show, a restaurant reservation or other personal requests you may require, he or she knows how to get it done. The more prestigious the hotel, the greater the sphere of influence they have to make it happen. Other professionals throughout the city know when they hear from the concierge of a fine hotel on behalf of a guest, that he or she is representing a real "player." The concierge can singularly make a difference in getting a reservation at those hard to get in "hot spots." Let them call on your behalf. The same is true if you're expecting more guests to arrive and your hotel is full. They usually have reciprocal relationships with other hotels of the same caliber. As a rule, a concierge prefers to be thanked after he/she has completed providing the service you have asked for. So, by all means begin your stay with an early introduction and then leave behind a sealed envelope or gift with his or her name on it. This expression of thank you will be long remembered.

The Bellman

This relationship is the most straightforward of almost all the hotel's staff. Basically, upon arrival, he will make sure your bags remain safe before you check in. A good bellman will try to insist that you carry nothing to your room. Upon opening the door, he will double-check your room's readiness and will

do almost everything except put your clothes away, and will do that as well, if you ask. As a practical matter, there's not much he can arrange other than calling the desk for certain arrival needs. However, later, if you need an errand to be run, he will be more than happy to oblige. If you are traveling alone, five dollars will do.

The Chambermaid

Don't be bashful about making your personal comforts known to your chambermaid. Extra daily towels, robes, shampoos or what time you like your bed turned down are just a few things she can arrange. As a rule, don't wait until the end of your stay to show appreciation. Five dollars in advance will say a lot about how you like your service.

The Doorman

Think of the doorman as your eyes and ears. He's like your own inside man! With that in mind, he can help you locate someone whom you really would like to find or bump into *on purpose*. This is your man for information! He sees the goings-on all day long. He also will arrange for a cab or any other local service you may require. Five dollars makes a nice introduction.

The Pool Man

Ah, the satisfying feeling of relaxation and comfort. Proper lounging by a pool requires more than just a chair and a towel. Like the restaurant reservation, *seating* is essential. You may not want to be near a rest room, or the kiddie pool. More importantly, you will want to take notice where the sun rises and sets so your lounge chair gets maximum sun. (Don't forget your sunscreen!)

Some of the finer hotels have private cabanas. The pool man can make those arrangements. It is a good idea to tele-phone him immediately upon arrival, or better yet, at the time you make your hotel reservations. Oftentimes reserv-ing a cabana is on a first-come-first-served basis. Some hotels charge a daily rate. Having a private cabana can make all the difference in the world when spending the whole day at the pool. Whether you'll be conducting business, spending time with your spouse or just need quiet time, be sure to ask if this service is available. Introduce yourself to the pool man and start him off with a fresh ten-dollar bill.

Chapter Twelve

TAXICABS

— *The Art of Hailing One*

Signal Method

On the Street

Anyone who's ever been in a major downtown city, such as Chicago or New York, and tried to hail a cab with six other people waving frantically side by side, knows the value of using the Signal Method. This technique can make a real difference between getting a taxi or having to forget the whole thing and settle for a latté at Starbucks!

The street must be regarded as a jungle. The shortage of cabs, especially during a rainstorm, cold weather or a big convention, brings out the competitive nature in all of us as we wait with an eagle eye for the next lit light on a Yellow Cab. So don't rely on other people's goodwill and manners. Stay alert and always be on the lookout, trying to make eye contact with a driver. Most importantly, always have your money in full view with your hand held high as you signal the cab you have in sight. A taxi driver will more likely stop for someone waving a handful of bills than an empty waving hand! When the street is crowded it is also best to stand in the middle of the block where there are less people.

The Tag Method

Another unconventional method is called The Tag. Under certain circumstances try to partner with someone as they

are getting into a cab. You will need to move fast when you spot a person just opening the door of a cab! Ask the person what direction they're going in. You can say, "Do you mind if we split the fare?" Most people are reason-

able as well as practical in wanting to save money. Be sure to smile so the person doesn't feel threatened. The street is no place to be shy, especially if you really need to be somewhere quick!

The Doorman

One of the most frustrating experiences after coming out of a crowded hotel is standing with about 15 other people waiting for a cab. *Solution:* Identify the lead doorman. He is usually the person standing in the hotel driveway with a whistle, directing the cabs and opening the door for each patron. He's your man! Walk straight past the front of the line. Wait for the right moment (usually when he is open-ing the door for the next person in line) and greet him by whispering, "I'm from New York and will be happy to take care of you the *right way* if you would arrange for a taxi now for me." Then say: "Where would you like me to stand?" Tell him, "I know you are under tremendous pressure but I only have a few minutes to get to my next appointment." Again repeat, "I'll take care of you big time!" At this point use the Single Handshake Method and press his tip (no less than five dollars) in his palm. Chances are he will more than likely give you the proper instructions as to where to stand to get a cab. Most likely other people in line will be watching. However, by the time you complete your business, it will be too late for them to comment. Besides, it's not their comments you're interested in—it's getting a taxi! Don't be intimidated, tipping for success takes confidence!

Go to the main road just before the front of the hotel driveway and hail a cab using the Signal Method. Although cab drivers are instructed not to stop to pick passengers up on the road, they often will.

Driveway Technique

Here's another effective method for getting a taxi when there is a long line in front of a hotel: It's called the Driveway Technique. Go to the main road just before the front of the hotel driveway and hail a cab using the Signal Method. Although cab drivers are instructed not to stop to pick passengers up on the road, they often will. I have found that more than 50 percent of the cab drivers will stop and pick you up.

Airport Taxis

Taxi areas at airports have become more or less city regulated and it is particularly difficult to secure a cab ahead of

others in a long line. However, there are exceptions. If you've ever traveled to Las Vegas during a busy convention (like the Consumer Electronics Show or COMDEX (computer show), then you know the impossibility of getting a taxi upon arrival at McCarran Airport. More than any other city in the world, Las Vegas conventions have attendance exceeding 250,000 people. A wait could easily exceed one hour! So here's a tip. Find a skycap, even if you don't have luggage, and let him know *you will be happy to take care of him in a big way* if he will get a taxi for you. At that airport, skycaps are given priority for cab services and even have their own taxi areas roped off just for them. The tip should be at least five dollars. More than worth it!

Three Ways of Sharing a Cab

Here are three pointers that don't require any tipping when you discover a long line of people waiting:

1. Share a cab. Ask the people further up the line if they are going near your destination and, if so, whether they'd like to share a ride to save money. If they say yes, then you can comfortably join them at the front of the line. Don't be embarrassed to announce your destination in a loud voice.

2. *Multiple taxi lines.* At many airports, most of the taxi stands are fed via two-way radio from a central taxi waiting area. However, at some airports, some taxi stands are fed from a separate dispatch. If your taxi stand has a long line of passengers and even fewer taxis, you're probably better off going to another taxi stand area.

3. *The less-crowded terminal.* If you know well in advance that a particular airline or terminal is likely to be more crowded, you might want to consider walking to another terminal. This also holds true for the majority of major city airports and their neighboring regional airports.

Chapter Thirteen

VALET PARKING
— How to Not Wait

Sometimes waiting too long for your car after a great dinner or meeting, or anything else for that matter, can be an obnoxious reminder of how tiring it can be to travel and wait, even locally! Other times, what might ordinarily be a small nuisance can be embarrassing and stressful if your time is limited and you must be somewhere quickly. Fortunately, most people really don't mind being relegated to milling around at curbside for up to 20 minutes, waiting for their car to be brought up. However, if you're not one of those people (and good for you), the methods discussed here, when properly followed, will prevent a lot of frustration and wasted time.

Keeping Your Car Up Front

There should be two objectives when arriving at valet parking: First, your car should remain up front so you get it faster and, second, you should not have to carry around that "little cardboard" ticket stub to retrieve your car. Sometimes not having to deal with little things can make a big difference. How many times have you left a restaurant, walked over to the valet attendant, reached into your pocket (or purse) for

The secret to not allowing the attendant to give you the stub is to remain steadfast with an attitude that you do not hold parking stubs.

that "little stub," only to find you have misplaced it. After turning your pockets inside out you scurry back inside the restaurant searching for it. If you don't find it, then the process to prove that your Volvo is really yours can make you feel like you're at a police line up.

No Ticket Method

It works like this: When you get out of your car and the attendant is preparing to hand you the parking stub, you very confidently and with a smile hold up your hand as if to stay *stop—*

and at the same time shake your head *no.* Say nothing at first! This signals to him that somehow you are a "regular" or at the very least more familiar than he is with certain "exception" procedures. The only time this may not work is if the attendant is in fact the manager of the entire concession. Then, he may insist on giving you a ticket. But still, that is unlikely.

The secret to not allowing the attendant to give you the stub is to remain steadfast with an attitude that you do not hold parking stubs. Period! Like anything else you do well, you must have genuine self-confidence. As the attendant makes another attempt to hand you the ticket stub, again you continue to subtly *shake your head no* with your hand raised as if to say stop. At this point, only about 15 or 20 seconds have gone by (I know it seems longer). If he still insists, you tell him, "I will be happy to take care of you later and would prefer if my car were left up front. I need to leave quickly when I finish." If he still insists, tell him with a casual but firm tone, "Don't worry, I'll take care of you." In all my experience, I have never been refused when requesting the No Ticket Method. The entire transaction should take about 30 seconds. As an additional touch, sometimes it can help if you continue to move toward the front entrance of where you're going. Don't walk too fast, as this can be taken as a sign of disrespect. Your body language sends three messages: First, that you don't

Your body language sends three messages: First, that you don't have time to deal with "a ticket," second, you know exactly where you are going, and third, somehow you have done this before.

have time to deal with "a ticket," second, you know exactly where you are going, and third, somehow you have done this before. Most parking attendants, when confronted with this method, will almost appear frozen in their tracks impressed by the unusualness of your behavior as well as by your confidence.

The Long Line

If for some reason you are unsuccessful in applying the No Ticket Method and find yourself standing in a line ten people deep waiting to redeem your car, don't give up. You've got another chance to show your skills! As you see a valet attendant driving up, meet him near that car and wait for the proper moment to catch him alone. Tell him you are in a spot and *will take care of him in a big way* if he will bring up your car up RIGHT AWAY! Most times he will accommodate. For a little extra insurance, use the Advance Tip Method. On the rare occasion where the attendant is unable to comply, ask him where the supervisor on duty is (don't forget to get his name first). Find that person and tell him (using his first name) the exact same thing you told the valet. Watch the speed at which your car appears. He most likely worked his way up the ladder to become manager learning the lessons of efficiency and the value his customers place on not waiting.

How much to tip is a matter of judgment. A five or ten dollar bill depending upon the circumstances is just the touch.

The Car Check Technique

An Added Time Saving Jewel

Here's a great time saving idea that I mentioned earlier if you're using valet service at a restaurant. It's worth repeating again in full. When your waiter brings the check, hand him your valet parking stub and ask, "Would you please be so kind to give this to the valet attendant outside. I'm in a bit of a hurry tonight." Tell him this with confidence, but *not* arrogantly. You want him to get the feeling you've done this many times. At first your waiter may be surprised at such an unusual request, but very quickly you will see a genuine willingness to accommodate. The reason is quite simple. The timing of asking him to do this will be at the same time you are reviewing your bill and adding the tip. Your waiter will be very aware of this. Don't worry if some- how you are unable to coordinate this timing. Chances are he will still do it, as long as you've treated him respectfully throughout his service.

The obvious reason to ask at the time you're finalizing your bill is that in another few minutes you'll be getting up and putting on your coat to leave. In those five minutes, until you make your way out of the restaurant, he will have already handed the attendant your parking stub so your car will be in front. **The result:** No waiting and no hassles! This is a real jewel of a service and one of the best kept secrets for those in the know! Having your waiter do this does not require an extra tip. Be generous once and it will go a long way.

Chapter Fourteen

AIRPORTS AND SKYCAPS

With the increased security and new federal regulations at airports, there are fewer opportunities to speed up what can sometimes feel like an eter-nity when checking in your luggage or standing in line for ticketing. However, there are still ways to accelerate service.

Skycaps

You're running late and your flight departs in ten minutes. You've missed the 20-minute cutoff time for baggage check in. That means, if you're lucky enough to make the flight, your bags may not! Forget the customary tip of a dollar a bag. If minutes count, use the Signal Method *(page 68)*. Hold up a handful of bills as you catch the eye of a skycap to handle your bags. If you think that's too aggressive, consider arriving without your bags or, worse, getting back in line and missing your flight.

As an alternative, and just as effective, go directly up to a skycap (while he is tagging another passenger's luggage) and whisper to him just how prepared you are to take care of him. I usually use the Advance Tip Method here. Mention his name if he is wearing a nametag and quietly press a ten-dollar bill in his palm, telling him, "Roger, there's ten dollars for you. I'm in a spot and minutes count. I'm on flight 602 to Miami. Thanks for taking care of me." Be sure to mention your flight number and destination.

This can feel uncomfortable considering others may be watching or even listening. However you must keep in mind

the consequences of either missing your flight or arriving without your luggage. This is a great motivating factor! Do not retreat! Remain steadfast on your mission. Help is on the way. Tipping for success requires confi-

dence in your purpose and sustained energy. People who watch you navigate successfully may look a bit annoyed, but privately may be thinking, "I wish I knew how to do that."

Ticketing

Do not fly ticketless! Always ask for a printed ticket when booking your reservations. The "Ticketless" method of traveling is fast becoming very common. True, it's easy and convenient, with one less thing to remember to take, but the consequences for not having a printed ticket in the event of certain problems isn't worth the risk!

Here are three reasons why:

1. Most importantly, if your flight is delayed or canceled and you want to change airlines, you'll need the actual printed ticket for another airline to honor your purchased ticket. Worse yet, you'll have to stand in line all over again (that could take over an hour) just to get a printed ticket from your original carrier. You'll need the printed ticket for another airline to get reimbursed from your original carrier. As soon as you figure out there might be a problem with the airline you're traveling on, ask any agent what other airlines have exchange agreements that will take your ticket. Even better is to know this information at the time that you make your reservation. If weather problems are the reasons for all flight delays, with the possibility of being socked in for the night, immediately call the nearest hotel (with shuttle service) to book a room as back-up. They fill up quick! Stay ahead of the bad news curve.

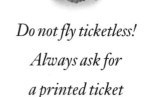

Do not fly ticketless! Always ask for a printed ticket when booking your reservations.

2. The second reason for not traveling ticketless is to insure that you have one less line to stand in at check in. With a preprinted ticket and seat assignment, you're on your way to boarding immediately.

3. The third reason, although less frequent but worth a try, is when you're running late or get pulled over by the police and have to show proof of why you're going so fast. Police officers and others recognize more quickly a printed ticket than a crumpled fax copy. Still, you will have to tell a tale to convince them (the truth is good) but at least they'll believe that you really have a flight to catch!

Getting Upgraded

Nowhere are passenger manners and etiquette more highly

respected by airline personnel than at ticket counters. So if you're looking for a freebie or favor, be on your best behavior. Free upgrades (other than when an agent or airline is at fault and wants to make it up to you) are at the sole discretion of your ticket or gate agent. I remember reading the following story that illustrates perfectly how not to act! To the credit of this very wise agent, she chose to diffuse through humor a seriously disruptive passenger.

During a very crowded boarding process at United Airlines, a single agent was calling for last-minute standbys. Suddenly, an angry passenger pushed his way to the front of the line. He slapped a ticket down on the counter and said, "I have to be on this flight and it has to be first class!" The agent replied, "I am sorry, sir, I must help these people who were here first and will do my best to help you as well." The passenger was unimpressed. He asked loudly (so the passengers behind him could hear), "Do you have any idea who I am?" Without hesitating, the ticket agent picked up the PA microphone and spoke with a loud concern. "May I have your attention please? "We have a passenger here at gate #27 who does not know who he is. If anyone can help this man find his identity please come to gate #27." Needless to say the entire gate was hysterical with laughter and the passenger eventually retreated to a place of embarrassment and humility.

Remember to be empathetic to ticket agents by letting them know you realize the pressure they are under in accommodating so many people. Never demand or demean! Here's another suggestion: If you are

Here's another suggestion: although ticket and gate agents are instructed not to accept money, they do appreciate other expressions of gratitude.

waiting to see whether or not an agent will be able to accommodate you (often they need 15 or 20 minutes to make something happen), bring back a cup of coffee or tea and place it on the counter. Don't make a fuss and don't hover! Just smile and say thanks. Also, whenever possible, ask for ' the supervisor in charge. They really have all the authority to make something happen.

Although ticket and gate agents are instructed not to accept money, they do appreciate other expressions of gratitude. This would be a good time to quietly offer a Tip Gift.

For example, you might present special gift certificates, movie passes or even the promise of sending something special in the mail. Recently on a trip back from Boston where I was wait listed, I spoke with the supervisor in charge. I asked where she was based and told her (off to the side of the gate), that if there was anyway she could help me get on that flight, I would arrange a first class facial at the Beverly Hills Hotel for her. This suggestion was just the right touch. I could tell she was stressed out from the flight being over sold. Still, thirty minutes later I heard my name called and got my boarding pass. I wasted no time the next day sending out that $85.00 certificate. More than worth it!

Always ask what percentage a flight takes off on time when making your reservation. Most major airlines keep a current database of take-off and landing activity for all their flights. They are 95 percent accurate.

Be creative. These Tip Gifts will be received as a kind expression of thoughtfulness. I always keep a few credit card size gift certificates from the Gap stores in my wallet when I'm traveling. They are the perfect size to carry. Other ways include the promise of sending something special in the mail.

Many airlines want their agents to be rewarded and have special coupons they mail to their frequent flyer customers, to give out to their agents who provide "extra level of service and comforts." These ticket agents receive special consideration from their airline company after accumulating a certain amount of these coupons. Try being aware of other passengers who may be within earshot when you suggest these goodies. Remember, think stealth. You certainly never want to put an agent at risk or on the spot if others are listening. One suggestion, track down a supervisor and ask, "Can we talk privately for a moment?"

Making Airline Reservations by Phone

If at first you're told the flight you want is "full" and you're not pressed at that moment to get a confirmed reservation , hang-up and call back 30 minutes later. Do this throughout the day.

You have at least a 50/50 chance that one of those calls will coincide with a cancellation and that phone agent will say— "We've got one seat left, shall I book it?"

Before confirming your reservation, here's a tip that can help you evaluate *on time departures* and arrivals. Always ask what percentage a flight takes off on time when making your reservation. Most major airlines keep a current database of take-off and landing activity for all

If you have a reserved seat and are involuntarily bumped, each carrier, according to federal regulations, is required to book you on the next flight or get you a comparable ticket on a competing airline.

their flights. They are 95 percent accurate. So, if you know ahead of time you have a connecting flight and learn that particular flight has been 65 percent late on arrival, you may want to seriously consider another flight or airline.

Prices

As a rule, making reservations by telephone will not yield you your best rate. Travel agents are still your most reliable source for getting lower fares. They have relationships with the airlines, and if you are off by one or two days, on a one-week advance notice, they can usually make that go away. In sharp contrast to working with a well-connected travel agent, there is very little you can say to influence an airline telephone agent. They are mostly scripted, and their software won't allow them to fudge the rate or reservation if it does not meet your need. At the very least, be sure you ask, "Is this your lowest fare?" or "Are there any other discounts available?" This may seem obvious, but telephone operators will usually NOT volunteer their best rate unless you ask. An alternate solution might be to book through an Internet discount web site. It can save you significant money. Airlines know this, and are now aggressively marketing their own online campaign, selling last minute "unsold seats."

What to Know About Getting Bumped and Long Delays

If you have a reserved seat and are involuntarily bumped, each carrier, according to federal regulations, is required to book you on the next flight or get you a comparable ticket on a competing airline. Compensation for this inconvenience is equal to the price of your one-way fare purchased ticket, or up to a maximum of $200. If your bumped flight delays you by more than two hours, you can ask for twice the value of your one-way fare or up to a maximum of $400. Some airlines may even let you keep your original ticket for future use.

If you think the long delay you are facing may be for reasons other than air traffic congestion or severe weather problems, immediately ask for the supervisor in charge. Maintain a calm, confident and informed manner as you ask to be booked on the next flight out on a competing airline. Supervisors and ticket agents know this regulation policy. Use it! Move quickly and confidently, but never arrogantly. You should also be aware that if there are no other acceptable flights out, your airline (according to carrier regulations) must refund your ticket even if it's a non-refundable ticket.

Very few airport hotels are actually in the airport. Some are as much as 15 miles away from the nearest terminal.

How to Increase Your Chances of Standby

Occasionally, if you miss your flight or show up last minute without a ticket and need to go stand-by, you should immediately take one or more of the following steps:

1. If the line is too long, go immediately to the nearest phone and make a reservation on the next flight out. Don't forget to use your cell phone if the wall phones or

pay phones have too long a line. You'll be surprised how many times you'll get through and get a seat. You can also use your cell phone at the same time you hold your position in line.

2. Hand the gate agent your ticket, since that will determine your standby priority.

3. Ask for a supervisor and don't be shy about letting her know how grateful you can be if somehow she can get you on that flight. Don't forget, you're a full-standing member in the Tipping for Success Club.

4. If you feel you need to, ask the gate agent to provide you with a written statement of their boarding priorities. By law, in the U.S., airlines are required to provide you with a written statement of their boarding priorities. However, do not act arrogant or pushy. Look in the policy statement and see if there is anything that could conceivably apply to you or your family. Generally, the U.S. airlines deny boarding on a last-come-first-bumped basis. However, many make exceptions. For example, airlines will give preference in those instances and to the extent such passengers would suffer an undue hardship such as the old, the handicapped, the infirm, infants, etc. A few airlines will give preferences to first-class, business-class and connecting passengers. Those airlines, which have the general undue-hardship provision, usually have a clause to the effect that business emergencies will not qualify as an undue hardship. Beyond that, the definition is up to the gate agent. In practice, an undue hardship usually

means a family emergency, such as seeing a dying relative or attending a funeral.

Be Careful About So-Called Airport Hotels

Watch out! Very few airport hotels are actually in the airport. Some are as much as 15 miles away from the nearest terminal. Be careful of misleading information with respect to advertised airport hotels. Only a few, such as Miami International, the O'Hare Hilton and the Sheraton Gateway in Toronto, Canada, are really within walking distance of the terminals.

Most airport hotels give a free bus ride in a van or automated transit system to get you to their hotel. For that reason, when choosing among airport hotels, be sure to ask exactly how far away each hotel is from the terminal. It could mean the difference between spending an hour waiting for a hotel van to arrive, or waiting for the driver to circle the airport a few times to pick up more passengers! Oftentimes free is no bargain at all. If you know that an airport has horrendous public transportation, plan in advance and have a town car waiting for you!

Chapter Fifteen

CAR RENTALS

Reservations

Little can be done to influence reservations agents to give you a car they do not have, or more commonly, a car reserved for someone else. The best you can do is to assure the agent that you will take any car, literally. Tell them it doesn't have to be fully cleaned, gassed or the latest model. Never push your luck if they offer you transportation that does not meet your lifestyle standards. Just visualize the alternative and you will see yourself quickly becoming very grateful. As a last effort, ask for the supervisor in charge, introduce yourself in a discreet setting and use the Advance Tip Method ($20 will do nicely), and ask again if he could check his inventory. Mention you'll see him again on your return and would be very grateful. Smile and say thank you!

Drive to the Gate Technique

When You're in a Hurry!

It's 2:45pm and your flight is at 3:10. You're just now pulling up to the car rental return. There's no way to check in your car, catch a shuttle to the gate and make the flight! Right? Wrong! The first thing you do when you arrive at the car  rental is *not* to go inside to the counter. Flag one of the people who check in the cars using the Signal Method and tell them you'll take care of them New York style if they will drive you to your gate right now! Because minutes count, you don't want to waste time if the person gives you resistance. Immediately go to the next check-in guy or gal and ask if they would like to make a *big* tip (one of the few times it's okay to say this) by driving you to the gate. If you're turned down again, try the third guy or gal and promise the same thing. Chances are one of the check-in attendants will take you up on your offer.

As a last resort you can also go inside and speak to management. Do this only as a last resort. Many rental companies allow their people to do this. As a matter of fact (this is off the record), some companies have VIP door to gate service.

Little Secrets about Renting a Car

1. **Join the car rental company's executive club system.** When you arrive to pick up your booked car, your information will allow you to bypass the lines at the terminal counter and go directly to an express desk at the lot. Some systems are even faster. When you arrive at the airport, you go straight to your rental car (bypassing the rental counter) finding your keys and the

completed rental contract sitting on the seat. All you need do is sign the contract, give a copy to the guard at the gate, and you're on your way.

2. **Choose a less popular rental car company.** The major delay in getting a rental car comes from excess passenger demand. In other words, no cars and at the very least, longer check-in lines. These problems can be avoided if you take the time to choose the lesser-known rental car companies. Although an off-airport rental car company will take a little longer to get to, it could be worth it considering the alternative of having no reservation and winding up with no car at all.

*The first thing you do when you arrive at the car rental is **not** to go inside to the counter. Flag one of the people who check in the cars using the Signal Method and tell them you'll take care of them New York style if they will drive you to your gate right now!*

Chapter Sixteen

NIGHTCLUBS

— *Getting In*

Most nightclubs or after-dinner nightspots are not private and usually will not take a reservation in advance. Part of their marketing strategy is to create a little sidewalk tension so that people will gather early and form a line. Line formation sends a tremendous advertising message, "This club is hot"! There are two strategies for gaining access to a club at the last minute: the Telephone and the Last-Minute Walk-In. These are basically the same strategies used for restaurants and hotels. *(See Chapters Ten and Eleven).*

Typically, nightclubs have two people managing the front door—a *Bouncer* and a *Doorman*. The nature of this kind of business requires such security. It's the doorman who generally makes the decision as to who gets in and who doesn't. When you find yourself waiting in a line that's no longer tolerable, approach the doorman as you introduce yourself, (looking very self-assured) and say, "Can I speak with you privately?" If he's unable to leave his post, immediately use the Double Handshake Method as you press a ten-dollar bill into his hand and discreetly say, "Hi Steve, I'm Bob Martin. Can you see what you can do to take care of

"You. You. And you."

my party of four? Thank you."

If you find yourself calling by cell phone, use the same methods found in earlier chapters. Be sure you know the name of the club manager first before calling.

Chapter Seventeen

Everyday Opportunities

By now I'm sure you can see how being a *confident and successful tipper* makes our daily life easier and less stressful. Service professionals, who go the extra mile for us every day, doing those little things, really do appreciate an unexpected thank you tip. Such is the case with our regular deliverymen, apartment doorman, garbage men, postman, gas station attendants, even our supermarket managers who manage to keep in stock our favorite brands of ice cream or yogurt. Most service professionals, whom we interact with on a regular basis, should be acknowledged more than the *once per year holiday perk.* This doesn't mean we have to tip each time they provide a special service. It does mean that for all their care and consideration (assuming that is what you are receiving), it's best to show our appreciation from time to time by doing something special like giving a tip gift.

Perhaps the most overlooked working professional when it comes to tipping (other than special holidays) are the receptionists, secretaries, assistants and the like who are really the gatekeepers that schedule so many of our important appointments. This certainly includes your family dentist or doctor. When you're in need of a last-minute appointment, sending a periodic "thank you gift," goes a long way in expressing your appreciation. By sending candy, flowers, gift certificate coupons, or muffins delivered in the morning with a note that says *thanks for fitting me in*, helps in a big way the next time you need a *quick* visit. The result of your spontaneous thoughtfulness, like any relationship, will be appreciated and remembered.

Chapter Eighteen

At Your Service

—*Advice from Service Professionals*

Almost all restaurant maitre d's, valet parking attendants, hotel concierges, waiters, supervisors and most other personal service professionals consider themselves, in a way, the proprietors of their own *Personal Service Business.* Just as important, each employee is also expected to provide satisfying service on behalf of his or her employer. However, it is also true that every service professional has the additional latitude and authority to offer a little something extra when it comes to personal service. Those additional services at the discretion of the person in charge define a part of what Professional Service Providers (PSP) can do. In this context, every such exchange is a business transaction, and if you think of it that way, you'll spend a lot less time standing in long lines.

Today, the term service provider has been inextricably linked to the Internet. We hear about ISPs (Internet Service Providers), ASPs (Application Service Providers), and MSPs

(Music Service Providers), to name a few. However, for more than 100 years there were, and still are, the original PSPs,

or Professional Service Providers. They remain the front line in the billion-dollar hotel, restaurant and travel industries.

On the following pages, you will hear from some of the most respected service professionals in these industries. You will also hear from other everyday PSPs from around the country and what they think about being *at your service.*

"I really appreciate when a customer takes into account my circumstances before asking me to do a favor for him. I also find it much more personal and genuine when a customer remembers to call me by my first name. I always try to make it a point to remember a customer's face and name who has taken the time to show his appreciation with a tip. Sometimes I can tell when a customer is nervous, almost as though this is his first time tipping to get extra service. I like helping out, kind of like giving him his first right of passage."

—**Eric Fialkowski,** *Maitre d', Mortons Restaurant*
Beverly Hills, California

"Guests often ask me what is an appropriate tip for a concierge. I prefer not to make an equation out of tipping. There are so many kinds of services. It's uncomfortable when guests place money in front of you upon their arrival before any services are performed. The most gracious way of tipping is for the guest, upon departure, to leave an envelope with the concierge's name on it. Some people offer gifts instead, such as a nice bottle of wine, etc. This is perfectly acceptable and also appreciated, just as is the simple expression, 'Thank you very much.'"

Ron Palmtag, *Chief Concierge, Park Hyatt San Francisco*
Board of Directors, Les Clefs d'Or
San Francisco, California

"My business is helping people get to where they have to go. I'll do whatever I can in my power to help make that happen. I don't like people to say they will take care of me—and then don't—just to get what they want."

Donnie Alpert, *Lead Doorman, Mirage*
Las Vegas, Nevada

"Most of the people I see everyday I know I will never see again. I also know that I am helping them in more ways than they realize. I like to be appreciated as more than just a bag handler. I handle many times their worldly possessions and try my very best to be sure their luggage arrives at the same time they do. The pressure starts at check in."

M. Ganter, *Sky Cap, American Airlines,*
Chicago's O'Hare Airport

"My policy is to try to accommodate all guests. However, if there are certain 'pocket tables' that become available, my discretion as to who I give it to is determined by the manners I have been shown. I am always grateful when a patron extends his appreciation through a gratuity."

Daniel Kennedy, *Director of Restaurants, The Pierre*
New York, New York

"While I work equally hard to please all my customers and make them feel comfortable, I must say that those patrons who are more gracious and thoughtful, I remember a little better."

Mitch Rosen, *Belvedere Manager, The Peninsula Hotel*
Beverly Hills, California

"Tipping a concierge is appreciated. It is especially appreciated when a concierge has enhanced your experience or made plans beyond the standard reconfirmation."

Holly Stiel, *Hollyspeaks.com*
Former Chief Concierge, Grand Hyatt Hotel on Union Square
Author & Trainer for the Concierge Industry

"I have always believed in tipping etiquette. It really is an art. In my twenty years of service in this field, I see a trend toward younger customers not knowing about tipping etiquette. It makes me feel uncomfortable and embarrassed when a patron unwittingly waves money at me, expecting a special accommodation."

Maurice Cohen, *Maitre d', The Bistro Garden*
Studio City, California

"I am always surprised (but ready) to give the different kinds of services my guests ask for. I remember one time, a first-time guest asked me to pick up a dress shirt at a local department store for him. He didn't make as big a deal about the name brand as he did in being sure it was a new white dress shirt that would be delivered to his room at exactly 5:45pm. It worked out well for both of us."

S. Allonster, Manager, Holiday Inn Express
Miami, Florida

"It is always a great surprise when my regular customers treat me to something special. I take great pride in making sure they get their deliveries on time and with the service they ask for. Sure I like to be appreciated."

Roland Oster, *UPS Driver*
Los Angeles, California

"One of the most stressful parts of my job is when flights get backed up and I announce delays at the gate. All of a sudden I feel like a target for 250 passengers who want something extra for the delay. I really do try to go out of my way for passengers who let me know in a quiet but confident way a good reason to upgrade them. I never do it for a reward, but it's a nice surprise if it does happen. The best surprise I ever got were tickets to CATS, for helping a businessman get on a very heavily booked flight."

T. Lester, *Ticket Agent, United Airlines*
New York, New York

"Many people think we leave the most expensive cars up front to show off a higher image and therefore make a higher tip. The truth is, we will leave any model car up front if the driver asks us to and tips a little extra for this convenience."

Tino Tomasi, *Valet Parking*
Boston, Massachusetts

"I don't mind if a customer wants me to rush and drive fast to get him to his appointment. But I don't like it when they take their anger out on me when they are running late. It's my license, not theirs, that's at risk. When a passenger lets me know he appreciates me going faster, I like to hear exactly how much appreciation."

Ricardo Mona, Cab Driver
Miami Beach, Florida

"The best customers are the ones who know where they want to go and how fast they want to get there. I work on the idea if I do my job right, then the customer will take care me right. At the end of the month, my tips account for almost 25 percent of my income. That's why I really come through for my passengers."

Hank Ofin, *Cab Driver,*
New York, New York

Chapter Nineteen

THE HISTORY OF TIPPING

One would like to think that the custom of tipping originated in the capital of entrepreneurism, the United States. Tipping has been such a standard part of our daily lives for so many generations, you would assume that we have always handed over a few silver dollar coins for services in America. But, like everything else, there is always a story behind the custom. When the first settlers came ashore, (of this soon-to-be country) they started setting up businesses and keeping shop. However, these early settlers were not able to reward special service with a gratuity, since most had come from humble backgrounds and had been on the receiving end of tipping.

The actual practice of tipping can be traced back to England during the 16th Century. Brass urns with the inscription "To Insure Promptitude" were first placed in coffee houses and later in local pubs. The word TIP came from the first three letters of this inscribed expression. Interestingly, back then, the custom was to tip in advance.

As the influence of the European culture made its way to the United Sates, Americans began to embrace this new system. It was in the late 1800's that affluent Americans returned home from overseas, and began offering a simple gratuity for a job well done. Americans were so taken with the effect it had on both relationships and the work done, they began to invent more unusual situations for ways to tip.

Soon, Americans became the favorite tourists while traveling to foreign countries. To this day, most people around the world still believe that all Americans (based on their generosity) are rich!

Back around 1905, tipping had gotten a little out of hand. It seemed as though almost every profession had the expectation, that in the end, a tip would be waiting. The hardest hit was the traveling salesman. He could barely step outside his hotel room before he was at the mercy of the waiters, porters and hotel managers. Business for them was not good enough to sustain this expectation. In 1905, these salesmen formally organized under the name the Anti-Tipping Society of America and actually were successful in putting into legislation a law against the practice of tipping. Tipping reached a point of outrage. This anti-tipping law was passed in Iowa, Washington, Arkansas, Tennessee, South Carolina, Georgia and Mississippi. In 1919, like many new laws, it was challenged and judged unconstitutional. This ruling came just in time, as the wild Roaring Twenties became the rage and tipping once again became very popular. However, ten years later the Great Depression put a virtual end to this practice. Tipping practically ceased. It wasn't until World War II, when the economy was jump-started, that tipping found its way back into the hearts of Americans. With so many service men away, bartenders, waiters, porters and bellmen, etc., became very scarce and found themselves in a *supply and demand* situation. Now, for the first time they could pick and choose their favorite and highest tipping spots.

Today, with the exception of a few foreign countries, the practice of tipping is pervasive, respected and here to stay!

Chapter Twenty

INTERNATIONAL TIPPING CUSTOMS

 Like language, each country has its own custom and public acceptance of what is considered appropriate when it comes to tipping. To help with understanding the international customs and traditions, I recommend that you speak with your travel agent when making travel arrangements to verify the local and country customs. For example, in Japan tips should be wrapped in a special envelope, allowing the server to feel more respected while preserving greater privacy among co-workers.

Interestingly, as I mentioned earlier in Chapter Five, sometimes giving a special "gift tip" can make the ordinary tipping routine a bit more "special." People know it takes a greater personal effort to find and send a gift. It signals a much stronger appreciation and respect than any amount of money. In countries like Russia, Japan and China, you will find that sending gifts will have the most meaning to those who have helped you the most.

Also, as a rule of thumb, the standard 15 percent is still

the customary rate around the world where tipping is permitted. As a reminder, and so that you are more prepared, try to carry the necessary coins and currency of that foreign country, so you can better navigate through their airports and have quicker access to the taxis. If you would like a more detailed breakdown on most country customs I suggest browsing various internet travel sites or visiting www.concierge.com.

Putting It All Together

Congratulations on being one of a new breed of travelers that now understands the art of *Stealth Tipping—invisible to the onlooker while achieving your purpose!* As you find new ways of tipping to lessen the stress and remain more productive on your next trip for business or pleasure, get ready to receive a whole new world of attention. Now it's your turn!

There is no one strategy or method that applies to all circumstances. Your own good judgment and experience will be your compass. Here are the four basic steps to achieving each tipping mission.

1. Identify the person in charge

2. Find the proper setting

3. Know what to say

4. Select the right method for passing the tip

The following overview is a working framework and glossary to help you evaluate which tipping method(s) and strategies are appropriate to a particular situation.

Taxis

The Tag Method

Sharing a cab with someone who has just opened the door of their cab and is about to get in. *(page 94)*

Driveway Technique

Hailing a cab in front of the hotel driveway on the main road. *(page 95)*

Signal Method

Holding a handful of bills above your head to catch a service person's attention. *(page 68)*

Car Rentals

Drive to Gate Technique

Used when you're running late! The first thing you do when you arrive at the car rental is not to go inside to the counter. Flag down one of the people who check in cars using the Signal Method and tell them you'll take care of them New York style if they will drive you to your gate immediately! *(page 118)*

5 Methods for Passing the Tip

Single Handshake

Of all the tipping methods, this one is the most natural. It utilizes the universal handshake, which has the built-in surety of the "no tell" tip off. In places where many eyes may be watching, the Single Handshake is undetectable. *(page 64)*

Double Handshake

This style of handshake is used when you want to convey a real warmth and appreciation for the courtesy being shown to you. It has strong overtones. This method suggests that the tip in your hand is more than the usual amount, and it emphasizes the importance of your request. *(page 65)*

Peel Method

This method is primarily used for parking attendants and vendors. It is best to use multiple dollar bills folded in half and held in the left hand as the right hand peels off one bill at a time. It is counted in full view for the attendant to see. You can show a little flair with this method. *(page 66)*

Agent Method

This method is pure stealth. Whether at a hotel, restaurant or valet parking, this method employs the help of a second party who handles the transaction on behalf of the tipper. In the case of restaurants, the tipper enlists and instructs a second person (usually the one he or she is with) to speak to the maitre d' on his or her behalf. It helps create a mystique of authority and keeps the mystery of your identity, thus showing your importance and ability to delegate. *(page 67)*

Signal Method

The sole objective is to catch a service person's attention! This very effective method is surefire when hailing a taxi on a crowded street or catching the attention of a skycap. *(page 68)*

.

Pocket Tips

Like all new information, we need to use it to remember it. With that in mind, if you would like to have an impeccable credit-card-size summary of "key tipping expressions" and "techniques for passing the tip," log onto: *tippingforsuccess.com.* If you prefer, enclose $7 and send to: Brenmark House, 13333 Ventura Blvd., Sherman Oaks, California 91423 and we will be happy to send you "Pocket Tips" with our compliments.

As an added bonus, you will also receive a charter membership in *tippingforsuccess.com* along with the 15 most important travel telephone numbers and web sites you don't want to be without.